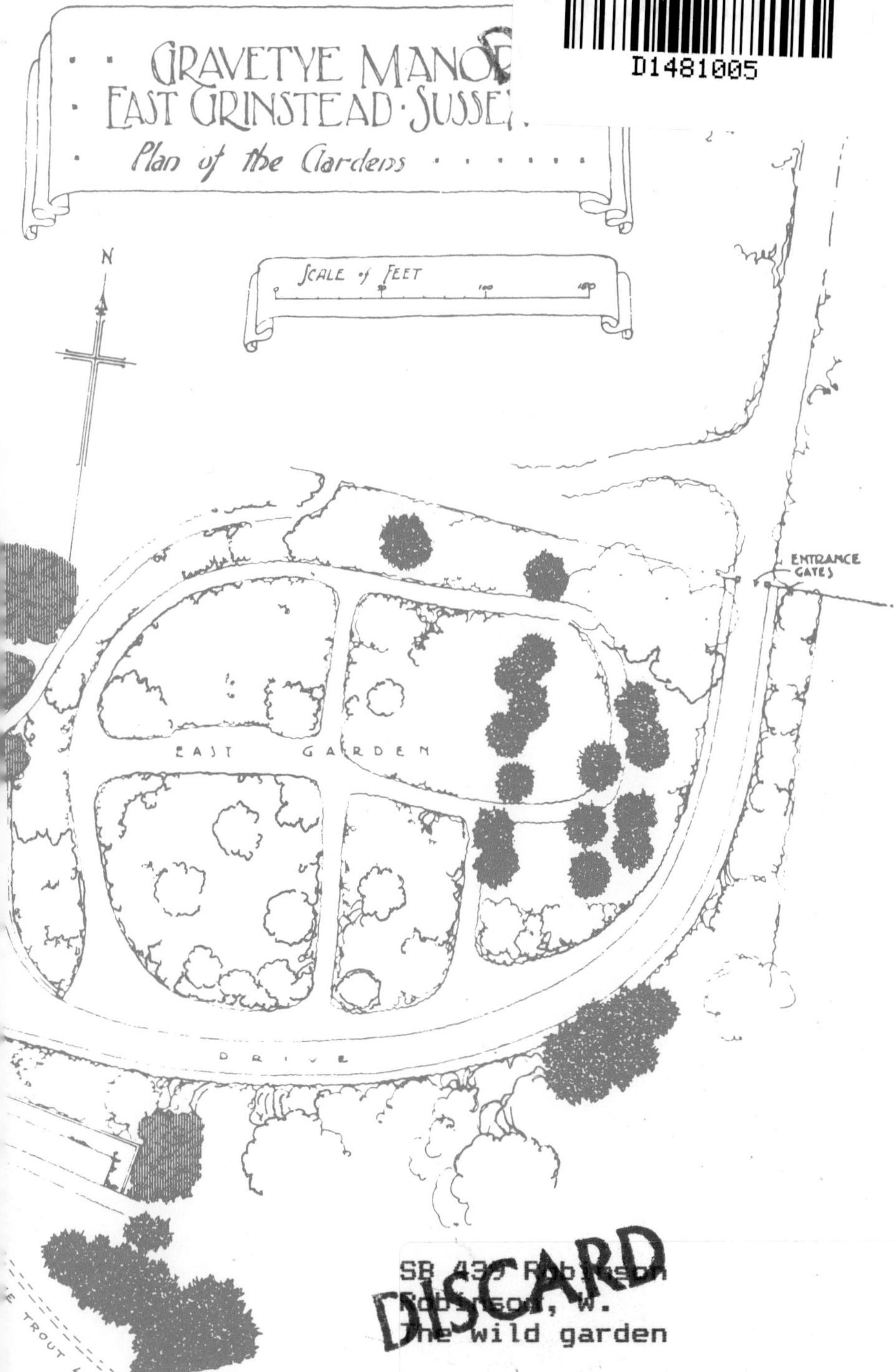

GRAVETYE MANOR
EAST GRINSTEAD · SUSSEX
Plan of the Gardens
SCALE of FEET
50
100
150
N
ENTRANCE GATES
EAST GARDEN
DRIVE
TROUT LAKE

THE WILD GARDEN

THE WILD GARDEN

by

WILLIAM ROBINSON

Foreword by
PETER HERBERT

Introduction by
JUDITH B. TANKARD

Botanical Revisions by
GRAHAM STUART THOMAS

A Ngaere Macray Book
Sagapress/Timber Press
Portland, Oregon

Endpapers map courtesy Gravetye Manor.

FRONTISPIECE: Combe in west country with primroses, kingcups, and daffodils. By Alfred Parsons, from *The Wild Garden,* Fifth Edition, 1895.

PAGE VI ILLUSTRATION: Gravetye Manor. By Alfred Parsons, reproduced with permission from *The English Flower Garden,* Fifteenth Edition, 1933.

Appendix II reproduced with permission from John Murray Publishers, London.

ISBN 0-88192-284-6

Printed in the United States of America

Sagapress, Inc. / Timber Press, Inc.
The Haseltine Building
133 S.W. Second Avenue, Suite 450
Portland, Oregon 97204-3527, U.S.A.

Library of Congress Cataloging-in-Publication Data

Robinson, W. (William), 1838–1935
    The wild garden / by William Robinson; foreword by Peter Herbert ; introduction by Judith B. Tankard; botanical revisions by Graham Stuart Thomas.
        p.   cm.
    Originally published; 5th ed. London: J. Murray, 1895. With new foreword and introd.
    Includes index.
    ISBN 0-88192-284-6
    1. Wild flower gardening. 2. Wild flower gardening—Great Britain. 3. Wild flowers—Great Britain. 4. Exotic plants—Great Britain. I. Title.
SB439.R62 1994   93-44917
635.9'676'0941—dc20   CIP

CONTENTS

FOREWORD
by Peter Herbert

WHEN WE CAME to Gravetye in 1958 the garden was a wilderness—a far cry from William Robinson's concept of a Wild Garden. As we progressed with the formidable task of clearing and restoration, it became clear that, mercifully, the bones of Robinson's garden remained intact.

Ironically, the survival of his garden was proof indeed of the principles put forward in this book—that plants hardy in our climate can be established, and thereafter left to fend for themselves. Prior to our arrival, no gardening had been practised for some three years; mature plantings of camellias had been covered by virile but invasive wisteria, groups of ericas were overwhelmed by brambles, but all survived. In contrast, the more 'artificial' flower beds in the gardens adjoining the house had succumbed totally to invasion by weeds, and the York stone paths had disappeared beneath a welter of uncut grasses of the coarsest kind.

The work of clearing alone took two years. During that time I discovered the writings of William Robinson. His name was barely recognised by the general public—only

eminent horticulturists such as my good friend Will Ing-
wersen, VMH, appreciated fully the contribution Robinson
had made to natural planting in the English garden. I
gained an understanding of his principles and concepts, and
began to follow his ideas, though not slavishly, in the
daunting task of refurbishing some thirty acres surrounding
the Manor. We have studiously avoided formality, and even
in the paved Flower Garden to the west of the Manor we
allow the herbaceous plants to tumble one into the other,
while clematis clambers freely over strong supporting roses
and hardy shrubs, trellis-work being eschewed. Robinson's
great sweeps of bamboo continue to dominate the Water
Garden adjoining the upper lake and the tall, stately polygonum, so invasive in a small garden, forms a bold stand
bounding the lake to the west.

The Alpine Meadow to the south of the Manor had
cared for itself most ably during the period of neglect. In
the spring it abounds with daffodils, with fritillaries, *Chionodoxa, Muscari* and *Colchicum* adding their sweeps of
colour through the seasons. All these, and many others,
were survivors in his Wild Garden from Robinson's time,
and have been supplemented by our plantings over the
years.

Thirty years on, we were content with our restoration;
then, on the night of 16 October 1987, the gardens were
devastated by The Great Storm. Some five hundred of our
trees fell in that one dreadful night—a stand of two hundred Corsican pines, the magnificent backcloth to the
Heath Garden, went down on our northern boundary. We

received overwhelming support from our hundreds of Country Club members, from English Heritage, from the Forestry Commission and, not least, from our small but magnificent team of gardeners, who initially worked night and day on the formidable task of clearance. The pundits have said that Nature simply did a clumsy job of pruning—we wish she had cleared away the resultant debris. But now, some years later, little sign remains of that devastation.

During the past three decades Gravetye Manor has, fortunately, become established and recognised as one of the leading Country House Hotels in Britain, and that success has enabled us to spend a veritable fortune on restoring and maintaining William Robinson's garden. We are proud that the many visitors to the Hotel and Restaurant are able to see his principles applied in their full glory. Had his gardens passed into oblivion through neglect, ignorance or lack of interest, we would only be able to read of them in his books. As it is, they remain a living and beautiful memorial to his vision.

INTRODUCTION
by Judith B. Tankard

THE LIFE and work of William Robinson (1838–1935) is not as well known as it should be, for he has been over-shadowed by his more famous contemporary Gertrude Jekyll, who designed several hundred gardens as well as wrote more than a dozen books. Because Robinson was not primarily a garden designer, his reputation lies mainly with his books, the best known of which is *The English Flower Garden.** This was the first book to popularise the use of hardy perennials in garden design, and earned him the nickname 'Father of the English Flower Garden'.

William Robinson was Irish by birth, but spent most of his life in West Sussex, where he lived at Gravetye Manor from 1885 until his death 50 years later. He was largely self-taught, his vast horticultural knowledge acquired through careful and deliberate study of plants in

---

*Reprinted by the Amaryllis Press (Sagapress, New York, and Hamlyn, London, 1984).

Britain, France, Switzerland and America. What distinguished Robinson from other horticulturists of the time was his ability to market his knowledge through books and periodicals. His colourful personality and sometimes outspoken temperament, combined with his editorial skills, exacting standards and financial acumen, led to an impressive list of publications for one lifetime. Although he remained a bachelor, his professional and personal acquaintances included such notable women as Gertrude Jekyll, Ellen Willmott and Viscountess Wolseley.

Robinson himself thought *The Wild Garden* one of his best books. This was due in part to his pleasure with the illustrations, by the artist Alfred Parsons, and with the quality of their reproduction in the book.[†] Originally published in 1870, *The Wild Garden* remained in print until Robinson's death in 1935. In some ways the book was more revolutionary than *The English Flower Garden*, as it treated a completely new type of gardening rather than catalogued existing ideas. *The Wild Garden* opened its readers' eyes to the natural beauty of indigenous wayside plants which were not part of the more structured garden areas that surrounded the house.

The subtitle he chose for the book varied with each edition until the fourth (1894), when he settled on 'The

---

[†]The numerous editions of *The English Flower Garden* were beset with all sorts of technical problems, which proved exasperating to the editor. See 'A Perennial Favourite: *The English Flower Garden*', in *Hortus* 17 (Spring 1991), pp. 74–85.

Naturalization and Natural Grouping of Hardy Exotic Plants'. The first edition offered 'Our Groves & Shrubberies made beautiful by the Naturalization of Hardy Exotic Plants', and the second (1881) further explained it as 'Being one way onwards from the Dark Ages of Flower Gardening, with suggestions for the Regeneration of the Bare Borders of the London Parks'. A chapter on British wild flowers in the original edition was dropped form the second and third, but restored to the fourth and subsequent editions. Robinson's habit of juggling with titles and chapters in all his books gave him plenty of freedom to express his ongoing thoughts on any topic. The fifth edition of *The Wild Garden*, now chosen for reprinting in facsimile, contains the selection of chapters that remained in print for the longest time (35 years), as well as the best reproductions of the illustrations.

Robinson's interest in the wild garden has sometimes been misinterpreted as an advocacy of natural landscapes of wilderness, rather than of landscapes enhanced by the use of carefree hardy, native plants. Writing in 1932 for the proposed eighth edition of *The Wild Garden*, Robinson returned to his original idea:

> As to the origin of my ideas of the Wild Garden, I think they first occurred to me along the banks of the Southern Railway between East Grinstead and West Hoathly. Sometimes when I went through the station I had a pocketful of seeds of some bush or plant which I used to

scatter about, usually forgetting all about them afterwards, but most certainly they all came up again.

Considering that this book was first published in 1870,
in the heyday of 'bedding-out', when hothouse-grown
exotic annuals were planted in geometrical or three-di-
mensional designs, it is astonishing that Robinson's ideas
should have been taken seriously. For the outer reaches
of larger country estates, he proposed the use of hardy
plants that would not only be carefree, but would natu-
ralise themselves. He popularised the idea of naturalised
stands of spring bulbs—anemones, narcissi, crocus—one
that is still considered appealing today. He also recom-
mended the use of groupings of native shrubs and trees
in the woodland. In addition to familiar wild flowers,
Robinson suggested that more striking plants, such as
cow parsnip, should have a place in the garden. Spe-
cialised plantings for hedgerows, copses, bogs and natural
rocky areas, 'not the absurdities too often made in gardens', were considered. Rereading *The Wild Garden* today, one is hard-pressed to name another book that treats
the subject better.

All the editions of *The English Flower Garden*, which
were aimed at more modest gardens, included a short
chapter on 'The Wild Garden' for those who had missed
that book, and Robinson continued to write about the
topic in his various periodicals. *The Wild Garden* was
very influential at the time. Both Gertrude Jekyll and the
American landscape architect Frederick Law Olmsted

owned copies, and Olmsted suggested that Calvert Vaux should follow the book carefully in laying out The Rambles in Central Park. There is no question that Miss Jekyll was profoundly influenced by the book. Her woodland garden at Munstead Wood was a living example of the principles of *The Wild Garden*. Here she had shrubbery-edge plantings of lilies and ferns, naturalised stands of foxglove in the woodland, and grass paths lined with trillium, bracken and dog's-tooth violets. She wrote that she 'always devoted the most careful consideration to any bit of wild gardening' and cautioned those 'unthinking people [who] rush to the conclusion that they can put any garden plants into any wild places, and that that is wild gardening'.‡

Robinson's first two books, *Gleanings from French Gardens* (1868) and *The Parks, Promenades and Gardens of Paris* (1869), had dealt with the lessons to be derived from French gardens. The year 1870 saw the publication of *Alpine Flowers for British Gardens* and *Mushroom Culture* as well as *The Wild Garden*. Prior to this, however, he had travelled to America. He met Olmsted and visited Central Park; in Massachusetts, he visited the famous pinetum at the Hunnewell Estate in Wellesley and Mount Auburn Cemetery, and met Asa Gray, the renowned botanist from Harvard University. He travelled by rail

---

‡*Wood and Garden*, p. 269 (Longmans, Green and Co., London, 1899; reprinted by Antique Collectors' Club, Woodbridge, Suffolk, 1981).

across the country, stopping in Baltimore and Chicago before reaching San Francisco. There he was reunited with his father, who had departed from Ireland under mysterious circumstances when William was a teenager. When he returned home, Robinson had enough capital to start *The Garden* magazine, first published in 1871.

Sometime after launching *The Garden*, he hit upon the idea of using illustrations by well-known artists to enhance both his books and his gardening magazines. He never used colour plates in his books, as he occasionally did in the magazines, but he had a critical eye for the artistic composition of the illustrations and the quality of the engravings. He used a variety of engravers—Kohl, Hyde, Huyot, Pannemaker—and their signatures are as prominent as those of the artists. In the production of his books he could be most particular, sometimes insisting that the engraver redo his work until he was satisfied. 'White Willow in Hampshire', one of the illustrations for *The Wild Garden*, was engraved three times. In a slightly unusual arrangement, Robinson closely supervised the engraving, printing and publishing of all his books until 1919, when he 'retired'. He personally selected engravers, printers and binders, and frequently complained that their work did not meet his precise requirements, but he left the imprint and distribution of the books to John Murray, the firm which worked with him for more than 60 years.

Occasionally Robinson thought that one of his books, having stood the test of time, deserved a special edition—*The Wild Garden* was one. In 1894 he had copies of the ordinary edition bound in soft vellum, with silk ties, possibly for private distribution. The next year he brought out a deluxe edition of the book from which the present facsimile is printed. The illustrations, which had been engraved in Paris, were printed on handmade paper from a French mill, and the book was bound in vellum with gilt decorations. The edition was limited to 280 copies which sold for a guinea (21 shillings) each, more than twice the price of his ordinary editions.

Robinson's deluxe edition was slow to sell, however. By 1920, when he was contemplating a new ordinary edition (which did not in fact appear until 1929), Murray cautiously suggested that the 74 remaining copies of the vellum edition, for which there was 'very little demand', should be sold off at cost before a new edition was embarked upon. Robinson agreed, and the edition was out of print by 1921. A final edition, with additional material (now published for the first time with the present facsimile as Appendix II), was contemplated by Robinson in 1932, more than 60 years after the initial publication of the book.

Over the years *The Wild Garden* was a steady seller, but the numbers would not please any publisher today: between 1914 and 1921, fewer than a dozen copies were sold in any year. Despite slim sales figures during the war, the book became one of Robinson's most successful titles. Not only did the topic continue to appeal to new generations of readers, but the book was attractively designed, further enhanced by the illustrations which first appeared in the second edition.

The artist, Alfred Parsons, RA (1847–1920), was a well-known painter, and President of the Royal Society of Painters in Water Colours. As a young man he gave up a career in the civil service to become an artist. In addition to painting, he illustrated numerous books, and the American publication *Harper's Magazine*. A bachelor, like Robinson, he was part of the 'Broadway Group' of artists who lived in Broadway, at that time part of Gloucestershire, since 1931 part of Worcestershire. His initial contact with Robinson may have been through his father, who was an expert on rock garden plants. Later, in 1895, he was one of four landscape painters who painted Robinson's new water-lily pond at Gravetye that summer. He also designed architectural modifications for the porch at Moat Cottage, near Gravetye.

Together with the artists Henry Moon, Edward William Cooke and Frank Miles, Parsons supplied illustrations for *The Garden* magazine, and some of these engravings were also published in early editions of *The English Flower Garden*, although the work is uncredited. Two of his illustrations appear in *God's Acre Beautiful* (1883). His best-known work was for Ellen Willmott's book, *The Genus Rosa*, also published by John Murray. Miss Willmott commissioned the paintings directly from Parsons, who had painted her own garden at Warley Place, Essex, but when she subsequently ran into scheduling and financial difficulties, both artist and publisher suffered. Parsons was particularly displeased with the reproductions.

There is no doubt that Parsons' working relationship with Robinson was much more satisfactory and enduring. With the exception of a couple of plant studies, such as '*Equisetum telmateia*', which were engraved from Gertrude Jekyll's photographs, Parsons provided all the artwork for *The Wild Garden*. In addition to numerous line drawings, the full-page paintings, such as the troublesome 'White Willow', are especially appealing.

Parsons was also a garden designer, and most of his work was carried out in the Broadway area. In addition to his own garden at Luggershill, he designed a garden with topiary peacocks at Court Farm, the home of Mary de Navarro, and gardens at Hartpury House which were later remodelled by the landscape architect Thomas Mawson. Mawson also followed Parsons at Wightwick Manor, Staffordshire, where he laid out a rose garden surrounded by clipped hedges and topiaried yews. Robinson, whose dislike of topiary and 'vegetable sculpture' was well known, cannot have appreciated Parsons' gardens. It is commendable that he should have selected Parsons as the illustrator for this very special book, and it is to be hoped that this new edition will bring pleasure to other generations of gardeners.

THE WILD GARDEN

Facsimile of the
Fifth Edition of 1895

THE WILD GARDEN

or the

Naturalization and Natural Grouping of
Hardy Exotic Plants with a Chapter on
the Garden of British Wild Flowers
By W. ROBINSON Author of
'The English Flower-Garden'
Fifth Edition
Illustrated by ALFRED PARSONS

'*Adspice quos submittat humus formosa colores*
Ut veniant hederae sponte sua melius'
<small>PROPERTIUS</small>

London   John Murray   Albemarle Street

m.dccc.xcv

I WENT to stay at a very grand and beautiful place in the country where the grounds are said to be laid out with consummate taste. For the first three or four days I was enchanted. It seemed so much better than Nature, that I began to wish the earth had been laid out according to the latest principles of improvement. In three days' time I was tired to death ; a Thistle, a heap of dead bushes, anything that wore the appearance of accident and want of intention was quite a relief. I used to escape from the made grounds and walk upon the adjacent goose common, where the cart ruts, gravel pits, bumps, coarse ungentlemanlike Grass, and all the varieties produced by neglect were a thousand times more gratifying.— SYDNEY SMITH.

INSCRIBED

TO

THE VERY REVEREND

S. REYNOLDS HOLE, D.D.

DEAN OF ROCHESTER

BY HIS FRIEND THE AUTHOR

CONTENTS

CHAPTER I.

CHAPTER II.

CHAPTER III.

CHAPTER IV.

CHAPTER V.

CHAPTER VI.

CHAPTER VII.

Contents

LIST OF ILLUSTRATIONS

COLUMBINES and GERANIUMS in meadow-grass.

PREFACE

————•◆————

WHEN I began, some years ago, to urge the cause of
the innumerable hardy flowers against the few tender
ones, put out in a formal way, the answer frequently
was, 'We cannot go back to the mixed border'—
that is to say, the old way of arranging flowers in
borders. Knowing, then, a little of the vast world of
plant beauty quite shut out of our gardens by the
'system' in vogue, I was led to consider some ways
in which it might be brought to our gardens; and
among them was the name and scope of the 'Wild
Garden.' I was led to think of the vast numbers
of beautiful hardy plants from other countries which

might be naturalized, with a very slight amount of trouble, in many situations in our plantations, fields, and woods—a world of delightful plant beauty that we might in these ways make happy around us. We can not only grow thus a thousandfold more lovely flowers than were seen in flower gardens, but also many which, by any other plan, have no chance of being seen in gardens.

In this edition, by the aid of drawings, I have tried to tell what the system is ;—if I were to write a book for every page that this contains, I could not suggest the many beautiful aspects of vegetation which the Wild Garden may give us.

The illustrations are, with a few exceptions, the work of Mr. Alfred Parsons, and the drawing and engraving have been several years in execution. They are after nature, in places where the ideas expressed in the first small edition of the book had been carried out, or where accident, as in the case of the beautiful group of Myrrh and white Harebells at Cambridge, had given rise to beautiful plant pictures. I cannot too heartily thank him for the skill which he devoted to the drawings, and for his success in showing the motive of the 'Wild Garden.'

There has been some misunderstanding as to the term 'Wild Garden.' It is applied essentially to the placing of perfectly hardy exotic plants under conditions where they will thrive without further care. It has nothing to do with the old idea of the 'Wilderness.' It does not mean the picturesque garden, for a garden may be highly picturesque, and yet in every part the result of ceaseless care.

What it does mean is best explained by the winter Aconite flowering under a grove of naked trees in February; by the Snowflake, tall and numerous in meadows by the Thames side; by the blue Lupine dyeing an islet with its purple in a Scotch river; and by the blue Apennine Anemone staining an English wood blue before the coming of our blue bells. Multiply these instances a thousandfold, given by many types of plants, from countries colder than ours, and one may get a just idea of the 'Wild Garden.' Some have thought of it as a garden run wild, or sowing annuals in a muddle; whereas it does not interfere with the regulation flower garden at all.

I wish it to be kept distinct in the mind from the various sorts of hardy plant cultivation in groups, beds, and borders, in which good gardening and good taste may produce many happy effects; distinct from the rock garden in its many aspects—all asking for skill and care; from the borders reserved for choice hardy flowers of all kinds; from the hardy sub-tropical garden or that of hardy plants of fine form; from the ordinary type of 'Spring Garden;' and from our

own beautiful native flowers, delightful in our woods
and fields and hedgerows. In country gardens, where,
on the outer fringes of the lawn, in grove, park,
copse, or by woodland walks or drives, there is often
ample room, fair gardens and new and beautiful
pictures may be formed by its means as the swift
springs and summers pass.

MAY 28, 1881.

A GOLDEN ROD.

LILIES coming up through carpet of WHITE ARABIS.

FOREWORDS TO NEW EDITION

THE wild rose has given her petals to the winds for over twenty summers since this book with its solitary wood-cut first saw the light, and if these many years give me any right to judge my own book, I may say that much experience since tells me that the 'Wild Garden' deserved to live, and that such ideas carried out with some regard to the soil and other things affecting plants in each place, may be fertile in making our open air gardens more artistic and delightful.

The best thing I have learnt from my own wild gardening is that we may grow without care many lovely early bulbs in the turf of meadows, i.e. fields mown for hay, without in the least interfering with the use of the fields.

The Blue Anemones, Crocus, Snowdrops, Narcisses, Snowflakes, Grape-Hyacinths, Dog's-tooth Violets, Stars of Bethlehem, Fritillaries, St. Bruno's Lily, Snow-glories, Wild Hyacinths, Scilla, and Wild Tulips best fitted for this early-gardening in the meadow turf, wither before the hay is ready for the scythe, and we do not find a trace of the leaves of many of them at hay time. Many of the plants of the mountains of central Europe and also of those of what we call the south and east, such as those of Greece and Asia Minor, bloom with me earlier than our own field or woodland flowers. Our feebler sun awakes them in the snowless fields, and so we enjoy many spring flowers while our grass is brown. And if they come so early in the cool and high 'forest range' in Sussex they will be no less early in the warm soils as in Surrey, or in the many valley soils—sheltered as they often are by groves and banks of evergreens. As nearly every country house is set in meadows it is easy to see what a gain this is, not only for its beauty but because it lets us make an end of the repeated digging up of the flower garden for the sake of a few annual and other spring flowers—themselves to be removed just in the loveliest summer days.

This spring I saw some evidence of what bold wild-gardening may give us in its effects on the beauty of landscape views. The picturesque view from Narrow-water House near Newry, across the park to the bay and the mountains that guard it, was much enhanced during March and the early part of the present spring by the great cloud of daffodils covering a mound in the foreground. The daffodils (the double kind so common in Ireland) spread over the mound in clouds, here and there massed close. It was not only good as a picture but as a lesson in the planting in the wild-garden of such flowers—which are often dotted about separately, much as fruit trees are in an orchard, instead of being held together in masses and bold groups, running out here and there into smaller ones.

Many of the reviewers of the book did not take the trouble necessary to see its true motive, and some of them confuse it with the picturesque garden, which may be formed in many costly ways, whereas the idea of the wild garden *is placing plants of other countries, as hardy as our hardiest wild flowers, in places where they will* flourish without further care or cost. *As I first used the word 'wild garden' in this book and in the '* Field' *newspaper, where some of the articles appeared many years ago, I wish to make its aim and meaning clear.*

I am happy to be able to illustrate the book with good wood engravings in these days of many 'processes,' often called 'improvements,' in book illustration, but which, so far, are its ruin. The few cuts done in the former edition by such processes have been re-engraved on wood for this. Some of the ideas in the book, such as the beautiful effects one may get in hedgerows and by grass-walks, are not illustrated as I hope they will be in future editions.

*As good examples of wild-gardening are likely often
to lie out of my own path, and as distinct and unlooked
for results will often arise, I should be grateful to all
who will tell me of them in the hope of making the
book more suggestive in future, as among the ways of
escape from the death-note of the pastry-cook's garden
there is none more delightful to all who have any grass
or fields or woods about them.*

W. R.

April 18, 1894.

SPIRÆAS, bushy and herbaceous.

THE WILD GARDEN

CHAPTER I.

EXPLANATORY.

ABOUT a generation ago a taste began
to be shown for placing numbers of tender plants in the open air in summer,
to produce showy masses of colour.
The plants were mostly from sub-
tropical lands ; placed annually in
the open air of our summer, and
in fresh earth, every year they
grew and flowered abundantly
until cut down by the first frosts.
The showy colour of this system
was very attractive, and
since its intro-
duction there
has been a gra-
dual rooting
out of all the
old favourites

LARGE FLOWERED MEADOW RUE : type of plant mostly excluded
from the Garden.

in favour of this 'bedding' system. This was carried to such an extent that it was not uncommon, indeed it was the rule, to find the largest gardens in the country without a single hardy flower, all energies being devoted to the few exotics for the summer decoration. It should be borne in mind that the expense for this system is an annual one; that no matter what may be spent in this way, or how many years may be devoted to perfecting it, the first sharp frost of November announces yet further labours.

Its highest results need hardly be described; they are seen in all our public gardens; our London and many other city parks show them in the shape of beds filled with vast quantities of flowers, covering the ground frequently in a showy way. I will not here enter into the question of the merits of this system; it is enough to state that even on its votaries it is beginning to pall. Some are looking back with regret to the old mixed-border gardens; others are endeavouring to soften the harshness of the bedding system by the introduction of fine-leaved plants, but all are agreed that a mistake has been made in destroying all our old flowers, from Lilies to Hepaticas, though few have a fair idea of the numbers of beautiful hardy plants which we may gather from every northern and temperate clime to grace our gardens under a more artistic system.

My object in the *Wild Garden* is now to show how we may have more of the varied beauty of hardy flowers than the most ardent admirer of the old style of garden ever dreams of, by naturalizing many beautiful plants of many regions of the earth in our fields, woods and copses, outer parts of pleasure grounds, and in neglected places in almost every kind of garden.

I allude not to the wood and brake flora of any one country, but to that which finds its home in the vast hill-fields of the whole northern world, and that of the hill-ground that falls in furrowed folds from beneath the hoary heads of all the great mountain chains of the world, whether they rise from hot Indian plains or green European pastures. The Palm and sacred Fig, as well as the Wheat and the Vine, are separated from the stemless plants that cushion under the snow for half the year, by a zone of hardier and not less beautiful life, varied as the breezes that whisper on the mountain sides, and as the rills that seam them. They are the Lilies, and Bluebells, and Foxgloves, and Irises, and Windflowers, and Columbines, and Violets, and Crane's-bills, and countless Pea-flowers, and Moon Daisies, and Brambles, and Cinquefoils, and Evening Primroses, and Clematis, and Honeysuckles, and Michaelmas Daisies, and Wood Hyacinths, and Daffodils, and Bindweeds, and Forget-me-nots, and blue Omphalodes, and Primroses, and Day Lilies, and Asphodels, and St. Bruno's Lilies, and the myriads of plants which form the flora of the northern or temperate regions of vast continents.

It is beyond the power of pen or pencil to picture the beauty of these plants. Innumerable and infinitely varied scenes occur in all northern and temperate regions, at many different elevations, the loveliness of which it is impossible to portray; the essential thing to bear in mind is that the plants that go to form them *are hardy, and will thrive in our climate as well as native plants.*

Such beauty may be realized in every wood and copse and shrubbery that screens our 'trim gardens.' Naturally our woods and wilds have no little loveliness in spring; we have here and there the Lily of the Valley and the Snowdrop, and everywhere the Primrose and Cowslip; the Bluebell and the Foxglove take possession of whole woods; but, with all our treasures in this way, we have no attractions in or near our gardens compared with what it is within our power to create. There are many countries, with winters colder than our own, that have a rich flora; and by choosing the hardiest exotics and planting them without the garden, we may form garden pictures. To some a plant in a free state is more charming than any garden denizen. It is taking care of itself; and, moreover, it is usually surrounded by some degree of graceful wild spray—the green above, and the moss or grass around.

Numbers of plants of the highest order of beauty may be at home in the spaces now devoted to rank grass and weeds, and by wood walks in our shrubberies.

Night effect of LARGE EVENING PRIMROSE in the Wild Garden (Œnothera Lamarckiana).

Among my reasons for thinking wild gardening worth practising by all who wish our gardens to be more artistic and delightful are the following :—

First, because hundreds of the finest hardy flowers will thrive much better in rough places than ever they did in the old-fashioned border. Even small plants, like the ivy-leaved Cyclamen, a beautiful plant that we rarely find in perfection in gardens, I have seen perfectly naturalized and spread all over the mossy surface of a thin wood.

Secondly, because they will look infinitely better than they ever did in formal beds, in consequence of fine-leaved plant, fern, and flower, and climber, grass and trailing shrub, relieving each other in delightful ways. Many arrangements will prove far more beautiful than any aspect of the old mixed border, or the ordinary type of modern flower-garden.

Thirdly, because no disagreeable effects result from decay. The raggedness of the old mixed border after the first flush of spring and early summer bloom had passed was intolerable to many, with its bundles of decayed stems tied to sticks. When Lilies are sparsely dotted through masses of shrubs, their flowers are admired more than if they were in isolated showy masses; when they pass out of bloom they are unnoticed amidst the vegetation, and not eyesores, as when in rigid unrelieved tufts in borders, &c. In a semi-wild state the beauty of a fine plant will show

when at its height; and when out of bloom it will
be followed by other kinds of beauty.

Fourthly, because it will enable us to grow many
plants that have never yet obtained
a place in our 'trim gardens.' I
mean plants which, not so showy
as many grown in gardens, are never
seen therein. The flowers of many
of these are of great beauty, especially
when seen in numbers.

A tuft of one of these
in a border may not
be thought worthy of
its place, while in some
wild glade, as a little
colony, grouped natur-
ally, its effect may be
exquisite. There are
many plants too that,

BLUE-FLOWERED COMPOSITE PLANT; fine foliage
and habit; type of noble plants excluded from
gardens. (Mulgedium Plumieri.)

grown in gardens, are no great aid to them—like the
Golden Rods, and other plants of the great order Compositæ, which merely overrun the choicer and more
beautiful border-flowers when planted amongst them.
These coarse plants would be quite at home in copses
and woody places, where their blossoms might be seen
or gathered in due season, and their vigorous vegetation
form a covert welcome to the game-preserver. To
these two groups might be added plants like the winter
Heliotrope, and many others which, while not without

use in the garden, are apt to become a nuisance there. For instance, the Great Japanese Knotworts (Polygonum) are certainly better planted outside of the flower-garden.

Fifthly, because we may in this way settle the question of the spring flower-garden. Many parts of every country garden, and many suburban ones, may be made alive with spring flowers, without interfering at least with the flower-beds near the house. The blue stars of the Apennine Anemone will be enjoyed better when the plant is taking care of itself, than in any conceivable formal arrangement. It is but one of hundreds of sweet spring flowers that will succeed perfectly in our fields, lawns, and woods. And so we may cease the dreadful practice of tearing up the flower-beds and leaving them like new-dug graves twice a year.

Sixthly, because there can be few more agreeable phases of communion with Nature than naturalizing the natives of countries in which we are infinitely more interested than in those of which greenhouse or stove plants are native. From the Roman ruin— home of many flowers, the mountains and prairies of the New World, the woods and meadows of all the great mountains of Europe; from Greece and Italy and Spain, from the hills of Asia Minor; from the alpine regions of the great continents—in a word, from almost every interesting region the traveller may bring seeds or plants, and establish near his

home living souvenirs of the various countries he
has visited. If anything we may bring may not
seem good enough for the garden autocrat of the
day, it may be easy to find a home for it in wood or
hedgerow ; I am fond of putting the wild species of
Clematis and other exotic climbers and flowers in
newly-formed hedgebanks.

Moreover, the great merit of permanence belongs
to this delightful phase of gardening. Select a rough
slope, and embellish it with groups of the hardiest
climbing plants,—say the Mountain Clematis from
Nepal, the sweet C. Flammula from Southern Europe,
'Virginian creepers,' various hardy vines, Jasmines,
Honeysuckles, and wild Roses and briers. Arranged
with some judgment at first, such a colony might
be left to take care of itself; time would but add to
its attractions.

Some have mistaken the idea of the wild garden
as a plan to get rid of all formality near the
house ; whereas it will restore to its true use the flower-
garden, now subjected to two tearings up a year—
i. e. in spring and autumn; as may be seen in nearly
all public and private gardens, in France as well as
in England—new patterns every autumn and every
spring—no rest or peace anywhere. In the beautiful
summer of 1893, the flower-beds in the public gardens
of Paris were quite bare of all flowers in June,
before the wretched winter-nursed flowers had been
set out in their patterns. If such things must be

done in the name of flower-gardening, it were many times better to carry them out in a place apart, rather than expose the foreground of a beautiful house or landscape to such disfigurement. Spring flowers are easily grown in multitudes away from the house, and, therefore, for their sakes the system of digging up the flower-beds twice a year need not be carried out. Wild gardening should go hand in hand with the thorough cultivation of the essential beds of the flower-garden around the house, and to their being filled with plants quite different from those we entrust to the crowded chances of turf or hedgerow:—to rare or tender plants

The MOUNTAIN CLEMATIS.

or choice garden flowers like the Tea Rose and Carnation—plants which often depend for their beauty on their double states, and for which rich soil and care and often protection are essential.

STAR OF BETHLEHEM in Grass.

CHAPTER II.

EXAMPLE FROM HARDY BULBS IN GRASS
OF LAWNS OR MEADOWS.

WE will now see what may be done with one type of vegetation—hardy bulbs like Daffodils and plants dying down after flowering early in the year, like the Winter Aconite and the Blood-root (Sanguinaria). How many of us enjoy the beauty which hardy Spring flowers of these orders might give us? How many get beyond the conventionalities of the flower-garden, with its patchings, and taking up, and drying, and playing with our beautiful Spring Bulbs? Garden adornment with early bulbs is merely in its infancy; at present we merely place a few of the showiest in geometrical lines. The little done leads to such poor results, that many people, alive to the charms of a garden too, scarcely notice Spring-flowering Bulbs

at all, regarding them as things which require endless
care, and as interfering with the 'bedding-out.' And
this is likely to be the case so long as the most
effective of all modes of arranging them is unused.

Look, for instance, at the wide and bare belts of
grass that wind in and around the shrubberies in
nearly every country place; frequently, they never
display a particle of plant-beauty, and are merely
places to be roughly mown now and then. But if
planted here and there with the Snowdrop, the blue
Anemone, Crocus, Scilla, and Winter Aconite, they
would in spring surpass in charms the gayest of
'spring gardens.' Cushioned among the grass, the
flowers would unfold prettier than they can in the
regulation sticky earth of a border; in the grass of
spring, their natural bed, they would look far better
than they ever do on the brown earth of a garden.
Once carefully planted, they—while an annual source
of the greatest interest—occasion no trouble whatever.

Their leaves die down so early in spring that they
would not interfere with the mowing of the grass,
and we should not attempt to mow the grass in such
places till the season of vernal flowers had passed.
Surely it is enough to have a portion of lawn as
smooth as a carpet at all times, without shaving off
the 'long and pleasant grass' of the other parts of
the grounds. It would indeed be worth while to
leave many parts of the grass unmown for the sake
of growing many beautiful plants in it. If in a spot

where a wide carpet of grass spreads out in the sheltered bay of a plantation, there be dotted the blue Apennine Anemone, any Snowdrops, the Snow-flake, Crocuses in variety, Scillas, Grape Hyacinths, many Narcissi, the Wood Ane-mone, and any other Spring flowers liking the soil, we should have a picture of vernal beauty, the flowers relieved by grass, and the whole devoid of man's weakness for tracing wall-paper patterns where everything should be varied and changeful. In such a garden it might be clear that the artist had caught the true meaning of Nature in her grouping, without sacrificing anything of value in the garden. *Mowing the grass once a fort-night in pleasure grounds, as now practised, is a costly mis-take.*

The association of exotic and British wild flowers in the Wild Garden. — The BELL-FLOWERED SCILLA, naturalized with our own WOOD HYACINTH.

We want shaven carpets of grass here and there, but what nonsense it is to shave it as often as foolish men shave their faces! There are indeed places where they boast of mowing forty acres! Who would not rather see the waving grass with countless flowers than a close surface without a blossom? Think of the labour wasted in this ridicu-lous work of cutting the heads off flowers and grass.

Let much of the grass grow till fit to cut for hay,
and we may enjoy in it a world of lovely flowers
that will blossom and perfect their growth before hay
time; some who have carried out the ideas of this
book have waving lawns of feathery grass where they
used to shave the grass every ten days; a cloud
of flowers where a daisy was not let peep.

It is not only to places in which shrubberies, and
plantations, and belts of grass in the rougher parts of
the pleasure ground, and moss-bordered walks occur
that these remarks apply. The suburban garden,
with its single fringe of planting, may show like
beauty, to some extent. It may have the Solomon's
Seal arching forth from a shady recess, behind tufts
of many Daffodils, while in every case there may
be fringes of strong and hardy flowers in the spring
sun.

The prettiest results are only attainable where the
grass need not be mown till nearly the time the
meadows are mown. Then we may have gardens
of Narcissi, such as no one dreamt of years ago;
such as no one ever thought possible in a garden.
In grass not mown at all we may even enjoy many
of the Lilies, and all the lovelier and more stately
bulbous flowers of the meadows and mountain lawns
of Europe, Asia, and America.

On a stretch of good grass which need not be
mown, and on fairly good soil in any part of our
country, beauty may be enjoyed such as has hitherto

only gladdened the heart of the rare wanderer on the high mountain lawns and copses, in May when the earth children laugh in multitudes on their mother's breast.

All planting in the grass should be in natural groups or prettily fringed colonies, growing to and fro as they like after planting. Lessons in this grouping are to be had in woods, copses, heaths, and meadows, by those who look about them as they go. At first many will find it difficult to get out of formal masses, but that may be got over by studying natural groupings of wild flowers. Once established, the plants soon begin to group themselves in pretty ways.

As further showing what may be done with the hardy bulbs, not only outside the flower-garden but even in what forms part of the farm, I print here a paper read by me before the Royal Horticultural Society in 1891.

EARLY FLOWERING BULBS IN MEADOW GRASS.

Having during the past five years planted several hundred thousand bulbs and roots in meadow grass, the results may, perhaps, be suggestive to others. An advantage of this method is the delightfully artistic arrangements of which it permits. It is also a deliverance of flower-beds from the poor thing known as spring bedding. This system of ' bedding,' which began

in France, and is there still seen in all its bareness,
spread to many of our gardens; it consisted of putting
out in formal masses a few biennial plants, such as the
Wood Forget-me-not and Silene. This necessitated
a complete change in the contents of the beds every
year, or, rather, twice a year, and therefore prevented
their being given to the nobler kinds of flower
gardening   It is easy to have all the flower-beds proper
devoted to precious and enduring plants, such as Tea
Roses, Carnations, and the plants that require good
and constant culture and time for development, by
the aid of the wild garden   We begin with the blue
Apennine Anemone: of this I planted several thousand roots in grass.   Not having any beds or borders
near the house where I wanted it, I put it in meadows
around the house in light broken groups and masses.
It flowers and increases every year without the slightest
attention; and, being early in growth as compared with
grass, disappears before the meadow grass has to be
cut in summer.   This is an important point, and
shows what may be done with many beautiful spring
flowers.   One has the pleasure of seeing them year by
year flowering in their seasons, and giving delightful
effects, as these Anemones did this year, both in groups
in the open sunny fields, and also clustering thickly
round the base of old Elm-trees on their margin.
Among the blue Anemone, here and there, stood
groups of Narcissus, and in cases where the Anemones
and Daffodils flowered together the effect was often

beautiful. This Anemone is hardy, and always grows freely in grass, and never deteriorates. In Greece this year I saw on the mountains acres of the blue Greek Anemone, and think it is equally as hardy and as free as the Italian one, and quite as useful for naturalization in the grass. The simplicity of the culture of plants like this, which thrive in meadow grass, and the foliage of which withers before the grass need be mown for hay, makes them a most important group, as so much meadow grass comes near most country houses. A very great number of the spring flowers of the northern world may be treated in this manner, and give us beautiful spring gardens.

The most important group of all these early flowers is the Narcissus. Five years ago I planted many thousands in the grass. I never doubted that I should succeed with them, but I did not know I should succeed nearly so well. They have thriven admirably, bloomed well and regularly, the flowers are large and handsome, and, to my surprise, have not diminished in size. In open, rich, heavy bottoms, along hedgerows, in quite open loamy fields, in every position I have tried them. They are delightful when seen near at hand, and also effective in the picture. The leaves ripen, disappear before mowing time comes, and do not in any way interfere with farming. The harrowing and rolling of the fields in the spring are a little against the foliage, and probably a better result could be obtained with the finer Narcissus by wood walks and open copses, which abound in so many English country places. With the great group of forms of the common English, Irish, and Scotch Daffodils I have had good results; they thrive better and the flowers are handsomer than in the wild plant—not uncommon in Sussex. The little Tenby Daffodil is very sturdy and pretty, and never fails us. The only one that has failed is the Bayonne Daffodil. A very delightful feature of the Narcissus meadow gardening is the way great groups follow each other in the fields. When the Star Narcissi begin to fade a little in their beauty the Poets follow, and as I write this paper we have the most beautiful picture I have ever seen in cultivation. Five years ago I cleared a little valley of various fences, and so opened a pretty view. Through the meadow runs a streamlet. We grouped the Poet's Narcissus near it, and through a grove of Oaks on a rising side of the field. We have had some beauty every year since; but this year, the plants having become established, or very happy for some other reason, the whole thing was a picture such as one might see in an Alpine valley! The flowers were large and beautiful when seen near at hand, and the effect in the distance delightful. This may, perhaps, serve to show that this kind of work will bring gardening into a line with art, and that the artist need not be for ever divorced from the garden by geometrical patterns which cannot possibly interest anybody accustomed to drawing beautiful forms and scenes. I need say no more to show the good qualities of this group of plants for wild gardening, many places having much greater advantages than mine for showing their beauty in the rich stretches of grass by pleasure-ground walks. Various kinds of places may be adorned by Narcissi in this way—meadows, woods, copses, wood walks, and drives through ornamental woodland and pleasure grounds, where the grass need not be mown until late in the summer.

Dog's-tooth Violet.—This beautiful and delicate-looking plant surprises me by the free way it grows in grass in several places where I have planted it, varying a good deal, according to the soil, in its size, but never failing to interest by its beautiful leaves and flowers. It withers rather early, and is a perfect plant for meadow culture.

Last autumn I made a trial of the Grape Hyacinth (Muscari), and was delighted with the result this spring, with the pretty clouds of blue, quite distinct in the grass

Snowdrops in various forms are indispensable, and do fairly well, though they vary very much in the way they thrive on different soils. They look much better in the grass than in bare earth.

Among the flowers in the meadow grass there is nothing more beautiful than the varieties of Snake's-head (Fritillaria). It is the very type of plant for this work, and the white and pretty purple flowers are admired by all who see them in the early grass.

The Crocus, from its early brilliancy, is indispensable,

and the hardier forms are able to take care of themselves. In all this kind of work, if we could get the wild types of plant it would be all the better, because such beauty as they possess is certainly never the result of cultivation. When we buy bulbs highly cultivated we may expect some reduction in the size of the flower when it assumes a semi-wild state ; but nobody who cares for the form and beauty of the flowers will mind this reduction. Flowers from bulbs planted several years are somewhat smaller than the newly planted kinds, but certainly no less beautiful. While we have proof enough that Crocuses grow well in meadow grass on a large scale, they seem particularly suitable for growing under groves of trees, their growth coming before the trees spread forth their leaves. In many country places outside the garden proper there are many spaces under trees often possessed by Goutweed and other weeds which should be given to the Crocus and like early flowers.

Tulips.— I have tried only one wild Tulip, the Wood Tulip (T. sylvestris), sent me from Touraine to the extent of a thousand roots, and I do not think we have lost any ; they bloom gracefully every year. The shortness of bloom which Tulips show should lead one to try the wild kinds in grass. Their broad, fragile leaves are apt to be injured by the harrow. They are better tried in copses or drives through woods, where they are free from this injury.

Stars of Bethlehem (Ornithogalum).—The starry trusses

of the common old border kind are quite different in effect from our other early flowers, and very pretty. In this genus there is much difference in habit, the greenish, drooping-flowered kinds, like *nutans*, giving quite a different effect from that of the common white border kind. There is no difficulty about growing these in grass.

The Snowflakes (Leucojum) do admirably, the early one being a more precious flower than the Snowdrop, useful to gather, and brightly effective very early. The later ones are also graceful things, free and handsome in rich grass.

Living in a world of Wood Hyacinths, there was less need to try the Scillas than the non-British flowers, which give us new aspects of flower life ; but so far the results have been good with the Spanish Scilla and the new Scilla-like plants (Chionodoxa), which are early and disappear early.

To this sort of flower-gardening, which extends so much the interest in flower life, the bulb merchants might do great good by offering such bulbs and roots as these at lowest possible rates by the thousand. It would pay cultivators to grow such roots in quantity for the public, as it now pays Lincolnshire farmers to grow the Snowdrop for the trade in that popular flower. The whole success of wild gardening depends on arranging bold, natural groups with a free hand.

Portion of field of POET'S NARCISSUS in bloom. Late variety, planted six years; soil cool loam. Meadow mown every year; plants never degenerating, but improving yearly, and showing much difference as to size and height according to rainfall. No preparation of the soil given, only turning up the sod, placing the bulbs beneath and replacing the turf.

4 Vol. 2c.

CHAPTER III.

CAUCASIAN COMFREY in shrubbery.

I WILL now try to show what may be done with one type of northern plants—the Forget-me-nots, one not so rich as others in plants for the wild garden. Through considering it, however, we may be able to form some idea of what we may do by choosing from all the plants that grow in the meadows and mountain-woods of Europe, Asia, and America.

The Forget-me-not family embraces a number of coarse weeds, but if it had only the common Forget-me-not, would have some claims on us; but what lovely exotic plants there are in this order that would afford delight if met with creeping about along our wood and shrubbery walks! Nature, say some, is sparing of her deep true blues; but there are obscure plants in this order that possess the deepest and most delicate of blues, and which will thrive in the wild garden. The creeping Omphalodes verna even surpasses the Forget-me-not in the depth and beauty of its blue, and runs about quite freely in any shrubbery or open wood, or even in turf in moist soil not very frequently mown. Besides, in the garden border, it would be a not very agreeable object when once the sweet spring bloom had passed ; whereas, in lanes, woods, or copses, the low plants are not noticed when out of flower, but live modestly till returning spring jewels them with the charm of fine colour.

Another plant of the order is so useful for this purpose, that if a root or two of it be planted in any shrubbery, it will soon run about, exterminate the weeds, and prove quite a lesson in wild gardening. I allude to the Caucasian Comfrey (Symphytum caucasicum), which grows about twenty inches high, and bears quantities of the loveliest blue pendulous flowers. It, like many others, does well in a grove, or shrubbery, filling in the naked spaces between the trees, and has a quick growth but never becomes weedy. As if to contrast with it, there is the deep crimson Bohemian Comfrey (S. bohemicum), which is sometimes startling from the depth of its vivid colouring ; and the White Comfrey (S. orientale), quite a vigorous-growing kind, blooming in spring.

These Comfreys, indeed, are admirable plants for rough places—the tall ones thriving in a ditch, and flowering better than they do in the garden in prim borders. There are about twenty species, mostly from Southern and Central Europe, Asia, and Siberia.

I should perhaps omit the British Forget-me-nots, wishing now chiefly to show what we may do with exotics quite as hardy as our own wildings, but where a British plant is not wild within the district in which we live, it may be brought into the wild garden with good effect. When I went to Gravetye Manor there was not a trace of the common water Forget-me-not there, in either of the two lakes or in the woodland streams that fed them. We had of course to get so good a plant for the garden to carpet moist beds; it grows very rapidly, and when the plants were thick the boys took baskets of them and threw them into the streamlets and round the margin of the ponds so that in a year we had delightful groups of the Forget-me-not by the water in many places, and as the ponds and streams of the place flow into the Medway river, no doubt seeds and plants were carried far down its banks. Also, as there was none of our beautiful wood Forget-me-not in the place, I sowed some in freshly sown turf and had the pleasure of seeing it bloom for many years. Thus we may not only introduce hardy exotic plants, but some fair flowers of our own country. How many garden waters do not show some of our handsomest native water plants, as the flowering Rush, great Buttercup, and Bog-bean? We have another Forget-me-not, not British, which surpasses them all—the early Myosotis dissitiflora This is like a patch of the bluest sky, before our own Forget-me-not has opened, and is admirable for banks in a wood or for moist stony slopes. In carting away the soil to put in the foundations of an addition to Gravetye house, many loads of rubbish were thrown in a heap in Warrens wood, where a year afterwards I came upon some beautiful tufts of this which had planted themselves from bits thrown out with the rubbish.

For rocky places and sandy banks we have the spreading Gromwell (Lithospermum prostratum) of a fine gentian-blue.

Good plants are the Lungworts (Pulmonaria), and often destroyed through exposure on bare dug and often dry borders. The old Pulmonaria (Mertensia virginica) is one of the loveliest of spring flowers. It is rare in gardens; if placed in a moist place near a stream, or in a peat or free sandy bottom, it will live; whereas it frequently dies in a garden. The newer and more easily grown Mertensia sibirica is a lovely plant, taller and loving a marshy place. These two plants alone would repay a trial in the wild garden and may show that for cultivation alone (apart from art, or arrangement) the wild-garden idea is sometimes worth carrying out.

Among annual flowers we have Borage, a few seeds of which scattered over fresh ground soon germinate, and form pretty patches.

The Cretan Borage is a curious old perennial,

seldom seen in gardens ; for its growth is robust and
its habit coarse. It is, however, a good plant for
a rough place where the ample room which it wants
may be spared and where it may take care of itself,
showing among the hardiest of the early spring
flowers.

THE CRETAN BORAGE (Borago Cretica), example of perennial too vigorous for flower-beds.

Thus, though I say little of the Alkanet (Anchusa)
tribe, several of which could be found worth a place
with our own British Evergreen Alkanet, it will be
seen that a garden of beauty may be reaped from
the Forget-me-not tribe alone. Any one could settle

the matter to his satisfaction in a couple of years with these plants alone, in a shrubbery, ditch, lane, or copse, always provided that he takes care to adapt each kind to the position and the soil. For instance, the Giant Comfrey will grow six feet high in rich or moist soil in a ditch, and therefore, once fairly started, might be trusted to take care of itself. The Caucasian Comfrey, on the other hand, grows from eighteen inches to two feet high, and is at home in the spaces in a copse or shrubbery. The creeping Forget-me-not (Omphalodes verna) is a little plant that creeps about in grass not over a span high, or forms a carpet of its own—these differences must be thought of, as without knowing something of the habits and stature of plants, mistakes will be made. These Borageworts, as rich in blue as the gentians, are often poor rusty things in exposed sunny borders, and much in the way when out of flower, whereas in shady lanes, copses, or shrubberies, in hedgerow-banks, or ditches, we only notice them in their beauty.

GROUP OF GLOBE FLOWERS (Trollius) in moist place: type of nobler
Northern flowers little cultivated in gardens.

CHAPTER IV.

EXAMPLE FROM THE GLOBE FLOWER ORDER.

THE Buttercup order of plants embraces many widely diverse in aspect from the common kinds that burnish our meadows. In it, for the Wild Garden, is the sweet-scented Virgin's Bower (Clematis flammula), a native of the south of Europe, but as hardy in all parts of Britain as our native Clematis. And as the Hawthorn sweetens the air of spring, so will this add fragrance to the autumnal months. It is never more beautiful than when crawling over some low tree or shrubs, and I have planted it in newly formed hedgerows. An open glade in a wood, or on shrubby banks near, would be charming for it, while in the pleasure ground it may be used as a creeper over old stumps or trees. The Hair Bell Virgin's Bower (Clematis campaniflora), and the beautiful white

Indian Clematis montana grandiflora, a native of
Nepaul, are as beautiful, and many others of the
family are worthy of a place, rambling over old
trees, bushes, hedgerows, or tangling over banks.
These single wild species of Clematis are more
graceful than the large hybrid kinds now common;
they are very hardy and free. In genial sea-shore
districts a beautiful pale kind, common in Algeria,
and in the islands and on the shores of the Mediterranean (Clematis cirrhosa), will be found charming—
nearly evergreen, and flowering very early in spring
—even in winter in some places and in mild years.

Next in this order we come to the Windflowers,
or Anemones, and more beautiful flowers do not
adorn this world of flowers. Have we a bit of
rich grass land not mown? If so, the beautiful
Alpine Anemones (A. alpina and A. sulphurea) may
be grown there, though they are rare and 'slow' to
establish. Any sunny bushy bank or slope to adorn
with charming early flowers? For this we have
Anemone blanda, a lovely Greek kind; place it in
open bare spots, as it is dwarf, and it will perhaps
at Christmas, and onward through the spring, open
its large blue starry flowers. The common Poppy
Anemone (A. coronaria) will be happiest in open,
bare, sandy or rocky places in loam; and the showy
scarlet Anemone will do best in rich but not heavy
soil. Of other Anemones, hardy, free, and beautiful
to run free in our shrubberies and pleasure grounds,

the Japan Anemone, its white varieties, and the Snowdrop Windflower (A. sylvestris), are among the best of the exotic species. The Japan Anemones grow so strongly that they will thrive even among stiff brushwood, brambles, &c.; and scattered along the low, tangled margins of shrubberies.

The WHITE JAPAN ANEMONE in the Wild Garden.

Few plants are more lovely in the wild garden than the White Japan Anemone and the various other tall Anemones of the same country. The wild garden is a home for numerous plants, to which people often begrudge room in their borders, such as the Golden Rods, Michaelmas Daisies, Compass plants, and a host of others, which are beautiful for a season only, or

perhaps too rampant for what are called choice borders and beds. This Anemone is one of the most
beautiful of garden flowers, and one which is as well
suited for the wild garden as the coarsest. Partial
shade seems to suit it; and in any case the effect of
the large white flowers is, if anything, more beautiful
in half-shady places. The flowers, too, are more
lasting here than where they are fully exposed.

As for the Apennine Anemone (the white as well
as the blue forms), it is one of the prettiest flowers
of any clime, and should be in every garden, in the
borders, and scattered in woods and shrubberies.
I have planted many thousands of it in various
soils, and it never fails, though it shows a great
difference in growth and freedom of bloom, according
to the soil, being much larger for example on warm free
Irish limestone soils than on cool soils in Sussex. But
it is so well worth growing everywhere that for it
alone it would be worth while to form a wild garden!
Near to it is the also beautiful blue Windflower of the
Greek hills, in effect like the blue Apennine Windflower, but more varied in size and colour in the south,
and in some of its forms earlier in bloom in spring. This
might perhaps not have the same love for the grass as
the Italian blue Anemone, but if not it would be easy
to naturalize in bare or stony places. The yellow
A. ranunculoides, a doubtful native, found in one or
two spots in England, but not really British, is strange
and charming but flowers well only on chalk.

The large Hungarian Hepatica (angulosa) grows freely among low shrubs and in half-shady spots, and we all know how readily the old Hepatica grows on garden soils of fair quality. There are many forms of the common Hepatica (Anemone Hepatica) grown in gardens, and all the colours of the species should be represented in every collection of spring flowers, where the soil is favourable to these plants, but Hepaticas are often evergreen plants, and being very dwarf ask for more care in naturalizing them than is needed for vigorous plants of the same order, some of which will hold their own among the coarsest weeds.

There are many of the Ranunculi, not natives of Britain, that would grow as freely as our native kinds. Many may remember the pretty button-like white flowers of the Fair Maids of France (Ranunculus aconitifolius fl. pl), in the old mixed border. This, and the wild form from which it comes—a frequent plant in alpine meadows—may also be enjoyed in our wild garden. Quite distinct from all these, and of charming beauty, is R. amplexicaulis, with flowers of pure white, and simple leaves of a glaucous green and graceful form ; a hardy and pretty plant on almost any soil. This is one of the elegant exotic forms of a family well represented in the golden type in our meadows, and therefore valuable as giving us a distinct form.

Of the Globe Flowers (Trollius), there are various kinds apart from the native one, all rich in colour and good in form. These are among the noblest wild-garden

ANEMONES in the Riviera.

plants—quite hardy, free of growth in the heaviest of soil and wettest of climates, a lovely type of early summer flower, and one distinct from any usually seen in our fields or gardens ; for these handsome Globe Flowers are among the many flowers that for years have found no place in the garden proper. They are lovely in groups or colonies, in cool grassy places, where many other plants would perish, but where they will get on well, even among docks or the coarsest native plants. I put them in wet hollows at Gravetye that no man could clear of weeds and had the pleasure of seeing their handsome flowers come instead.

The Winter Aconite (Eranthis hyemalis) should be naturalized quite under the branches of deciduous trees, will come up and flower when the trees are naked, will have its foliage developed before the leaves come on the trees, and be afterwards hidden from sight. Thus masses of this earliest flower may be grown without sacrifice of space, and will be noticed only when bearing a bloom on every little stem. On heavy soils it is not so free or bright as on free and limestone ones. That fine old plant, the Christmas Rose (Helleborus niger), likes partial shade better than full exposure, and should be used abundantly, giving it rather snug and warm positions, so that its flowers may be encouraged to open well and fully. Any other kinds may also be used. Recently many kinds of Helleborus have been added to our gardens ; and although all of them are not conspicuous as the Christmas Rose, yet they are of remarkable beauty of foliage and habit as well as of blossom, and they flower in the spring. These, too, show the advantage of the wild garden as regards cultivation. They will *do better in any bushy places, or copses or in mutually-sheltering groups on warm banks and slopes, even in hedge banks, old quarries, or rough mounds, than in the or-dinary garden border.* Of the difference in the effect in the two cases it is needless to speak.

THE GREEN HELLEBORE in the Wild Garden.

Some of the Monkshoods are handsome, but they are virulent poisons ; and, bearing in mind what fatal accidents have arisen from their use, they are better not used at all in the garden proper. Amongst tall and vigorous herbaceous plants few are more suitable for rough places. They are robust enough to grow any-where in shady or half-shady spots; and their tall spikes of blue flowers are very beautiful. An illustration in the chapter on the plants suited for the wild garden shows the common Aconite in a Somersetshire valley in company with the Butterbur and the Hemlock. The larger rich blue kinds, and the blue and white one, are showy grown in deep soils, in which they attain a great height. When out of flower, like many other stately perennials, they were often stiff and ugly in the old borders and beds ; in the wild garden their stately forms when flower-time is gone, no longer tied into bundles or cut in by the knife, will group finely with other vigorous herbaceous vegetation.

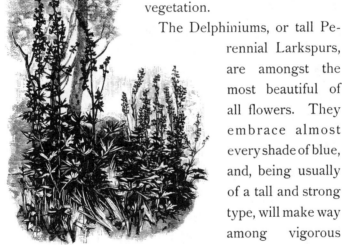

The Delphiniums, or tall Perennial Larkspurs, are amongst the most beautiful of all flowers. They embrace almost every shade of blue, and, being usually of a tall and strong type, will make way among vigorous weeds, unlike many things for which we

TALL PERENNIAL LARKSPURS, naturalized in Shrubbery (1878).

have to recommend an open space, or a wood with nothing but a carpet of moss under the trees.

One of the prettiest effects which I have seen was a colony of tall Larkspurs. Portions of old roots had been chopped off by the men when a bed of these plants was dug in the autumn, and the refuse thrown into a near plantation, far in among the shrubs and trees. Here they grew in half-open spaces, so far removed from the margin that they were not dug and were not seen. When I saw the Larkspurs in flower they were more beautiful than they are in borders or beds, not growing in such close stiff tufts, but mingling with and relieved by the trees above and the shrubs around. This case points out that one might make wild gardens from the mere parings and thinnings of the beds and borders in autumn in any place where there is a collection of good hardy plants

The engraving on the next page represents one of the most beautiful effects obtained in his wild garden by an acquaintance of mine who began when he knew very little of plants and their favoured haunts, and succeeded well in a not very favourable site. Herbaceous Pæonies were amongst those that succeeded best. The effect was very beautiful, either close at hand or seen at a considerable distance off. Herbaceous Pæonies are amongst the most free, vigorous, and hardy of perennial plants, and in free good soil with them alone most novel and beautiful effects may be carried out in most places where there is room. Even in small gardens, a group or two outside the margin of a shrubbery would be good. The effect of the blooms amongst the long grass is finer than any they present in borders, and when out of flower they are not in the way. It is almost needless

to speak here of the great variety of forms now obtainable amongst these Herbaceous Pæonies, the fine
double forms of which deserve the best cultivation in
beds and borders—the hardy free-growing wild kinds
will often come in for the wild garden. My friend's
Pæonies formed a group that could be seen from
a distance; when I saw them they were surrounded

DOUBLE CRIMSON PÆONIES in grass at Crowsley Park.

by long and waving grass. I cannot give any idea of
the fine effect.

The blue alpine Clematis-like Atragene alpina is one
of my favourite flowers—seldom seen out of a botanical
garden. It likes to trail over old stumps or through
bushes, or over rocky banks. Speaking of such plants
as this, one would like to draw a sharp distinction
between them and the various weedy and indistinct

subjects that are now creeping into cultivation owing to the revival of interest in hardy plants. Many of these have some botanical interest, but they can be only useless in the garden. Our chief danger now is getting into cultivation plants that are neither very distinct nor very beautiful, while perhaps we neglect many of the really fine kinds. This Atragene is a precious plant for low bush and bank wild gardening.

Among plants which one rarely sees in a flower-garden are the Meadow Rues; yet there is a quiet beauty about them. As some will grow often in a hedgerow or lane or byway, or in a copse, or under the shrubs, in places usually abandoned to common weeds, there is no reason why they should not be rescued from the oblivion of the botanic garden.

CHAPTER V.

PLANTS CHIEFLY FITTED FOR THE WILD GARDEN.

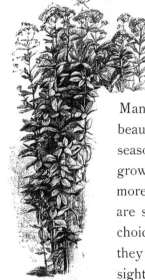

Type of erect COMPOSITÆ for the Wild Garden.

A GOOD reason for one form of the *Wild Garden* is that it offers us a way of growing a number of exotic plants not suited for garden culture in the old sense. Many of these plants have much beauty when in flower, and at other seasons, but they are so vigorous in growth that they overrun all their more delicate neighbours. Many, too, are so coarse that they are unfit for choice borders, and after flowering they leave a blank or a mass of unsightly stems. These plants are not pretty in gardens, and are a main cause of the neglect of hardy flowers; yet beautiful at certain stages. A tall Harebell, stiffly tied up in a garden border, is at best of times an unsightly object; but the same plant growing amongst the long grass in a thin wood is lovely. The Golden Rods and Michaelmas Daisies used to overrun the old mixed border, and were with it abolished. But these seen together in a New England wood in autumn are a picture. So also there are numerous exotic plants of which the individual flowers may not be so striking, but which, grown in colonies, afford beautiful aspects of vegetation. When I first wrote this book, not one of these plants was in cultivation outside botanic gardens. It was even considered by the best friends of hardy flowers a mistake to recommend them, for they knew that it was the mastery of these weedy vigorous plants that made people give up hardy flowers for the glare of bedding plants. The ' wild garden ' then, in the case of these particular plants, opens up to us a new world of infinite beauty. In it every plant vigorous enough not to require the care of the cultivator or

THE GIANT SCABIOUS (8 feet high). (Cephalaria procera.) Tall herbaceous plant, best fitted for the Wild Garden.

GIANT COW PARSNIP. Type of Great Siberian herbaceous vegetation.
For rough places only.

a choice place in the mixed border will find a home. Of such plants there are numbers in every northern country. The taller Yarrows, the stately Aconites, the vigorous, and at certain seasons handsome, Althæas, Angelica with its fine foliage, the herbaceous kinds of Aralia with fine foliage from the American woods, also the Wormwood family (Artemisia), the stronger kinds of American Cotton-weed (Asclepias), certain vigorous Asparagus, Starworts in great variety, Betonica, pretty, and with delicate flowers, but hardly fit for the mixed border, various vigorous Grasses, showy Buphthalmums, handsome Bindweeds, too free in a garden, the stout Campanulas, exotic Thistles, numerous Centaurea, somewhat too coarse for the garden ; and among other hardy plants, the following are chiefly suitable for the wild garden :

Crambe.	Helenium.	Rhaponticum.
Digitalis.	Helianthus.	Rheum.
Dipsacus.	Heracleum.	Rudbeckia.
Doronicum.	Inula.	Scolymus.
Echinops.	Lavatera.	Silphium.
Elymus.	Ligularia.	Solidago.
Epilobium.	Mulgedium.	Symphytum.
Eupatorium.	Onopordon.	Veratrum.
Ferula.	Phytolacca.	Verbascum.
Funkia.	Polygonum.	Vernonia.
Galega.		

CHAPTER VI.

DITCHES, SHADY LANES, COPSES, AND HEDGEROWS.

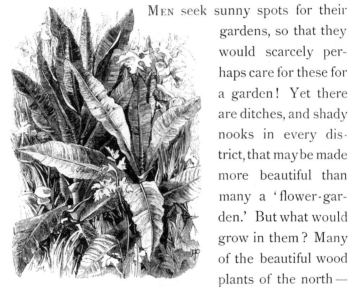

Foliage of TEAZLE, on hedge-bank in spring.

MEN seek sunny spots for their gardens, so that they would scarcely perhaps care for these for a garden! Yet there are ditches, and shady nooks in every district, that may be made more beautiful than many a 'flower-garden.' But what would grow in them? Many of the beautiful wood plants of the north — things that do not care for sunny hillsides or meadows, but take shelter in woods, or are happy deep between rocks, or in caves beneath the great boulders on many a mountain gorge, and garland the flanks of rock that guard the rivers on their way through the hills. And as these dark walls, ruined by ceaseless flow of the torrent, are often beautiful, so may we adorn the shady dykes and lanes. For while the nymph-gardener of the ravine may depend on the stray grains of seeds brought in the moss by the robin when building her nest, or on the mercy of the hurrying wave, we may place side by side the snowy white wood Lily (Trillium grandiflorum), whose home is in the shady American woods, the twin flower of Northern Europe, and find both thrive on the same spot. In North America in the woods and near them I often saw the wet ditches filled with noble ferns. And not only may we be assured that numbers of the most beautiful plants of other countries will thrive in deep ditches and in like positions, but also that not a few of them, such as the white wood Lily, will thrive much better in them than in the open garden, the results widely differing according to the nature of the soil and other things, the action of which is not always easy to understand. The Trillium has a flower as fair as any white lily, but, in consequence of being a shade-loving plant, it often perishes in a dry garden border, while in a shady moist dyke it will thrive as in its native woods ; and, if in moist, free soil, prove as fair as anything seen in our stoves.

Our wild flowers take possession of the hedges that seam the land, often draping them with such inimitable grace that half the conservatories in the country, with their small red pots, are poor compared with a few yards' length of the blossomy hedgerow verdure. Wild Roses, Purple Vetch, Honeysuckle, and Virgin's Bower, clamber above smaller, but not less pretty, wildings, and, throwing veils of graceful life over the hedgerow, remind us of the plant-life in the thickets of low shrubs on the Alpine meadows. Next to the most beautiful aspects of Alpine flowers, there are few things in plant-life more lovely than the delicate tracery of low-climbing things wedded to the shrubs in all northern and temperate regions. Often perishing like grass, they are safe in the earth's bosom in winter; in spring, finding the bushes once more enjoyable, they rush over them

THE LARGE WHITE BINDWEED. Type of nobler climbing plants, with annual stems. For hedgerows and shrubberies.

as children from school over a meadow of cowslips. Over bush, over brake, on mountain or lowland copse, holding on with delicate grasp, they engrave them-

selves on the mind as the type of graceful plant-life.
Besides climbing Pea-flowers and Convolvuli, of which
the stems perish in winter, we have the great tribes of
wild vines, noble in foliage, the many Honeysuckles,
from coral red to pale yellow, all beautiful; and the
Clematidæ, varied, and lovely, some with small flowers
borne in showers like drops from a fountain jet, and
often sweet as Hawthorn blossoms.

This climbing vegetation may be trained and tor-
tured into forms in gardens, but never will its beauty
be seen until we entrust to it the garlanding of shrub,
and copse, or hedgerow, fringes of plantation, or
groups of shrubs and trees. All that need be done
is to put in a few tufts of a kind, and leave them
alone, adapting the plant to the spot and soil. The
large Hungarian Bindweed would be best in rough
places, out of the pale of the garden, so that its roots
might spread where they could do no harm, while a
fragile Clematis might grow over a tree and star its
green with fair flowers. In a wood we see a Honeysuckle clambering up through an old Hawthorn tree,
and then struggling with it as to which should give
most bloom—but in gardens not yet. Some may say
that this cannot be done in the garden, but it can be;
because, for gardens we can select plants from so many
countries, and adapt them to our particular wants and
soils. We can effect contrasts, in which nature is often
poor in one place, owing to the few plants that naturally
inhabit one spot of ground. Foolish old 'laws' laid

down by landscape-gardeners perpetuate the notion
that a garden is a 'work of art, and therefore we
must not attempt in it to imitate nature!' true gardening differing from all other arts in this that it
gives us the living things themselves,
and not merely representations of them
in paint or stone or wood.

Where there are bare slopes,
an excellent effect may be obtained by planting the stouter
climbers, such as the Vines,
Mountain Clematis, and Honeysuckles, in groups on the grass,
away from shrubs or low trees ;
while, when the banks are
precipitous or the rocks crop
forth, we may allow a curtain
of climbers to fall over them.

THE NOOTKA BRAMBLE. Type of free-
growing flowering shrub. For copses
and shrubbery.

Endless charming combina-
tions may be made in this
way in many spots near country houses. The
following are among the climbing and clinging
hardy plants most suitable for garlanding copses,
hedges, and thickets :—Everlasting Peas (many kinds),
the Honeysuckles, Clematis (wild species mainly), the
common Jasmine, Brambles, Vines (American and the
common varieties), single Roses, Virginian creepers
(Ampelopsis), the large Bindweed (Calystegia dahurica),
Aristolochia Sipho, and A. tomentosa, and several of the

perennial Tropæolums (T. pentaphyllum, speciosum, and tuberosum). The hardy Smilax and the Canadian Moonseed, too, are very handsome, and suitable for this kind of gardening.

Among the plants that are suitable for hedgerows and lanes, &c. are—Acanthus, Viola, both the sweet varieties and some of the large scentless kinds, Periwinkles, Speedwells, Globe Flowers, Trilliums, Plume Ferns (Struthiopteris), and many other kinds, the Lily of the Valley and its many varieties and allies, the Canadian Blood-root, Winter Greens (Pyrola), Solomon's Seal, and allied exotic species, May Apple, Orobus in variety, many Narcissi, the Common Myrrh, the perennial Lupin, hardy common Lilies, Snowflakes, Everlasting Peas and allied plants, admirable for scrambling through low hedges and over bushes, Windflowers, the taller and stronger kinds in lanes and hedgerows, the various Christmas Roses that will repay for shelter, the European and hardier kinds of Gladiolus, such as segetum and Colvillei, the taller and more vigorous Crane's-bills (Geranium), the Snake's-head (Fritillaria) in variety, wild Strawberries of any variety or species, Giant Fennels, Dog's-tooth Violets in spots bare in spring, the Winter Aconite, the May Flower, for sandy poor soil under trees, Toothworts (Dentaria), the 'coloured' forms of Primroses, 'Bunch' Primroses, Ox-lips, Polyanthus, the hardy European Cyclamens, Crocuses in places under trees not bearing leaves in spring, the yellow and pink Coronilla

(C. montana and C. varia), many of the taller Harebells, Starworts (Aster), the Monkshoods which people fear in gardens ; the different species of Allium often not welcome in gardens, some of which are beautiful, as, the White Provence kind and the old yellow garden Allium (Moly). With the above almost exclusively exotic things and our own wild flowers and ferns, beautiful colonies may be made.

When I first wrote the *Wild Garden*, it was to

THE YELLOW ALLIUM (A. Moly) naturalized.

encourage the gardener to put some beautiful life in his garden grass, shrubberies, and half waste places —if ashamed of that beautiful life among his Perilla and dark Beet and Alternanthera. But now I want the fields to be gardens too, since at Gravetye I found I could do so much in the meadows mown for hay. The *Wild Garden* I see now need not stop at the pleasure-ground fence. Among the ways one may enjoy it most is in the making of living fences. In our country the system of keeping stock in the open air, instead of in sheds, makes a fence a necessity as all know to their cost, who have to look after a country place or farm of any size. But we live in mechanical days, when many think that among the blessings and fine discoveries of the age is that of making a gridiron fence! and so we see some of the fairest landscapes disfigured by a network of iron fencing. And when a man throws away beautiful living fences and gives us miles of ugly iron in the foreground of a fair landscape, I think of the Devil setting up as an economist. Artistic, too, no doubt some of these improvers think themselves!

Iron Fences and our Landscapes.

The iron fence bids fair to ruin the beauty of the English landscape, unless men see its ugliness and its drawbacks as a fence, its great cost, and the further cost of tinkering and daubing it with tar or paint. With bullocks on one or both sides of an iron fence, its fragility as a fence is soon seen. It is no use as a shelter, nor as a protection, as it only forms a ladder for all who want to get over with ease. As a boundary fence it means the loss of all privacy. Estates of much natural beauty have their charms stolen away by iron fences. Used to fence the pleasure ground or by drives, the effect is bad to any one who knows how much more beautiful live fences are. There is nothing an iron fence does that an 'old-fashioned' one will not do better, while it always looks well with its Ivy, Ferns, Primroses, and varied life. The bad opinion of the old-fashioned fence arose from its being so often neglected, and injured by trees until no longer effective.

It is not only the tradesman emerging from the city who fancies there is no fence so perfect as an iron one. Such an idea would be excusable in mechanics, and many others who have not studied the question of fences from the point of safety, endurance, and beauty, and who fear the expense and trouble of forming a living fence. But I regret to see the plague of iron fencing in some of the finest country places and marring the foreground of good views.

No Fence so good as a live one on a bank.

One objection to the live fence is its weakness at first, and the need of protecting it when small, but these difficulties are not insurmountable. It is usual to plant Quick small, and then protect it with elaborate fencing on either side—wearisome work, for which there is no need if people would take the trouble to get plants strong enough to form a good fence to begin with. With stout Quick, and a mixture of Holly, or other strong bushes, a good fence can be made at once without protection being needed. In every country place it would be easy to have a few lines of young and vigorous Quick put out in fields in lines a yard or so apart, where they might get stout, and be ready for fencing at any time. Where there are underwoods with Quick growing in them, it is often easy to grub up bushes of it, cut them down half way, and plant them in a fence, always on a bank.

I have done this with success and without losing a bush, but should prefer to have a few lines of stout grown Quick ready to take up at any time. Most fences should be on banks with 'dicks' where the ground requires them, because the bank itself forms a fence against lambs and small animals, and the added soil that goes to make the bank gives much better growth. Three years ago I formed a fence of this sort, every bush of which was gathered in the underwood near ; the line of Quick was so strong that there was no need to fence them. To prevent, however, any chance of cattle rushing through, a thin Larch pole was run through along and just below the top of the fence, supported by the bushes, and no animal has since passed the fence or injured it. The waste slender tops of Larch lying in a wood near were used. This fence will be good for as many years as it is wanted, will form a shelter as well as a fence, and will not want any attention for many years to come. It should be clearly understood that in the formation of this fence we had not even the cost of the ordinary 'stake and heather' protection commonly used in re-making rough fences. The tough bushes did it all themselves, the sod bank helping them in all ways. Consider this as compared with the costly galvanized or iron fence, with its dangers, ugliness, and coldness!

By far the best fence for farm and general work is the living fence—the most satisfactory and least expensive in the long run, and the most beautiful in its effect upon the landscape and for its varied life. I mean the living fence that is not too trim, and annual trimming is not necessary. Small, ' skinny ' Quick fences are not so handsome as rough ones. The constant clipping of fences is needless in many grazing and woody districts. In good arable farms it may be desirable, but in most districts where fields are large the fence should also be a shelter — a bold, free-growing screen, with Bramble, wild Rose, Ferns, Ivy, and other scrambling things that like to live in it. I have many such fences that do not want attention for years at a time—on banks, as they always should be. They are better furnished at the bottom than some of the constantly clipped hedges. To plant on a bank may in some very dry soils, and where there is a low rainfall, be a mistake, but the bank itself doubles at least the depth of the soil, and the protection of the bank and its little dick is a great gain to fencing, by allowing Briers and wild Roses to fill in the bottom of the hedge, and preventing small animals from making tracks through. My fences round woods are only re-made when the underwood is cut, say every ten years, and that is sufficient. The mass of wood behind and the strong growth in the fence itself are such that no animal makes an attempt on them. The only source of weakness in such places is hedge trees, and they should be removed.

A hedge can be kept in good order for generations by cutting and laying it every ten or dozen years, and the owner of such a fence deserves to suffer if he does not take care that this is done when the time comes round. The labour for it is enormously less than the cost of forming and tarring the iron fence and keeping it in repair.

Bushes to use and avoid in Fences

To use bad fencing plants is folly, the money is thrown away, and the work never done. I have planted some thousands of Quick this season, in lines 3 feet apart, for the sake of getting strong bushes to make fences, and some Cockspur Thorn, of which I saw an excellent fence in France in 1892. I am not so sure about the Cherry Plum, which grows well in some places, but is not so tough as a Thorn, and in some cold soils, where the Quick is all we want, the Cherry Plum will not thrive. A few Sloe bushes may be used, but they are not so tough as Quick. A few seedling common Hollies not over 3 feet high are good, and, where there are not many rabbits to bark it, nothing is more successful than Holly. Hollies grow under trees better than any other fence plant. From the protection they give to stock, it is surprising that they are not more largely grown for shelter in stock-raising districts, and not clipped but grown naturally. One very often sees beautiful, almost natural fences of Holly and Quick in the forest districts of the south of England, and among Holly hedges well formed in better land, those at Woolverstone, in Suffolk, are excellent. Except, however, in open woodless districts where rabbits are few, Hollies are sure to be barked when rabbit food is scarce. I have planted several thousands within a few years, and none are intact that are not protected by wiring. Sweet Brier, Dog Rose, and cut-leaved Bramble are very good to mix, and beautiful too in a rough, wild-looking hedge.

It is as necessary to avoid bad fencing plants as to select and grow good ones. The worst is the common Privet, the ghost of what a fence plant should be. Its rapid growth deceives, and it is often used with a dangerous sharp-pointed iron fence outside as a guard, and perhaps, at the same time, to be the death of some animal. Privet is a rapid grower, or seems so at first; it is never so strong a grower in the end as Quick, Holly, or wild Rose. The quicker the Privet grows the worse it is, and the plant should never be seen in a fence. Laurel is a soft useless fence plant, apt to be killed in cold districts and in valleys. Spruce is sometimes used in hedgerows, and is most unfitted for them for many reasons. The common Elder is always a source of weakness in a fence, and should never be planted or allowed to live in a fence.

Oak and other not ugly Fencing.

Where there are beautiful views, people who enjoy the landscape will do well *not* to mar them with iron fencing. In some cases good views are kept by a sunk fence, and to prevent this from looking hard or deceptive in any way I throw a garland of wild Roses along the top of the wall, which marks the position of the fence, and always looks well. The groups of wild Roses I set out in a colony along the sunk fence made at Gravetye are charming at all seasons. In many other cases, along important drives perhaps commanding interesting views, a finer thing by far than any iron fencing is the strong split Oak post-and-rail fence. There are many estates where Oak is abundant, and where the men split it up into stout heartwood posts and rails. This is not necessarily a dear fence, and it is a very beautiful and efficient one if well done. In colour it is perfect, improving as it gets older. Such a visible tangible fence will last for many years, and might come in the foreground of a picture by Corot or Turner. A few Sweet Briers or wild Roses stuck in the post-holes often turn out very pretty. For dividing lines in stockyards, too, nothing is so good and safe as a split Oak fence. Where good effects are thought of, nothing is more important than good post-and-rail fences in certain places on the farm, where we want to keep animals back without hiding the view, and where shelter is not required. Oak park fencing is pretty, and in many cases efficient, but too expensive to be done on a large scale for field work. Nor should I rank it as high as a good live fence, because of its cost, repairs, and the quickness with which it is often destroyed when old.

The Fence as a Shelter.

Apart from the ugliness of the iron fencing, its giving no shelter whatever is one of its worst points, as a good live fence gives excellent shelter for sheep and other animals. The prim, neat little hedge is not so good as a shelter, but better than an iron fence. A well-grown fence, cut down and re-made after a lapse of say ten years, gives good shelter. There are many such shelter fences, with Holly and Thorn allowed to grow at will, with an interlacing of Ivy, all seated on a good bank. Such lines as these across the direction of the strong winds could not fail to be helpful for stock in exposed fields. We have plenty of materials to form such fences as hardy and enduring as the bank itself. We might even have them evergreen if we used the Holly largely. The shelter of a good line of naturally-grown Holly on the north side of a high field in an exposed district would be equal to that of a shed. There would be no great difficulty in establishing such Holly fences in open farming districts where rabbits do not abound, but it is not so easy in wooded districts Seedling plants, not large — i. e. 1 foot to 3 feet high —

are the best to use. It is a good plan to buy some
very small seedling Hollies, and let them get strong
in a nursery, so as to be able to get a few when
mending or making fences. The more ordinary
materials, too, with an occasional Holly intermixed,
give very efficient shelter indeed. The Ivy runs
through such fences and makes them very pretty,
tying them together with its graceful lace work, and
its growth seldom chokes the Quick or other plants.

The Fence Beautiful.

So far this about the true British fence is to lead
to what I want to emphasise—that the best and safest
live fence may be beautiful as well as enduring and
effective. If my reader will go so far as to form the
right fence, then he has it in his power to make
a very beautiful one, and to prove that use and beauty
are one even in a fence. Wild rough fences in many
countries are often pretty with Ivy, Clematis, Thorn,
Fern, wild Rose, Honeysuckle, Brier and Sloe, but
the trim clipped fence made of one sort of bush or
tree only is stupidly ugly. We may make fences
for miles, for ever beautiful yet always varied as one
goes along. But to do this one must never deviate
from the best fencing plants as a centre to the
fence—Quick, Holly, and Cockspur Thorn, and while
keeping to this central idea of the resisting and
enduring bushes, add what beauty we can, and that
is much! And as this is the *Wild Garden* its main

idea may well be kept in view; for though we may make a fence of beautiful native plants, fences in pretty positions near the house may be made more beautiful and interesting by adding perfectly hardy plants of other countries. It gives us a means of varying fences which is often surprising, and we may tie them together with graceful climbers which are not of our own country, though none surpass our Honeysuckle wreathed over a fence. I use Sweet Brier largely, and have for several years planted thousands in fence making. As this plant is not native in all parts of our country, it may be considered as worth introducing as any exotic! The odour from the early days of spring fills the field, and then there are the summer flowers, and the bright Hips for autumn and winter days. Its advantages are that cattle do not eat it, and that the flower or fruit-laden branches swing careless into the field, when Hazel and other things would be eaten back to the stump. The shoots are so fiercely armed with spines that cattle respect it, and it is a fine aid in live fence making. In building our fence some young Sweet Briers should be put alongside the bank, while Quick and the essential fencing plants that we may prefer for the spot go on the top The same thing applies to the wild Roses, the common Dog Rose of England being excellent. Other Roses will be found useful, such as the Japanese and the Needle Rose (R. acicularis). Different kinds of Bramble too are excellent, and often beautiful in

flower, fruit and leaf. There is great variety among
our Brambles, and not a few foreign ones are worth
introducing, if we can get them. Anyone who notices
English landscape beauty in spring will know how
much we gain from Crab and Sloe, and May Blossoms
in the fence. More beautiful things we cannot have,
but it is wise to add to them as we can in various
ways. Various bushes often abundant in gardens may
be introduced here and there. I have used some of
the dwarf Japan Crabs and Apples, the common Medlar,
the Quince, the Japan Pear, which in some places
comes so easily from seed, sowing the seeds on
banks as well as planting. The beautiful ' Pyracantha '
is a dwarf evergreen shrub, which I look forward to as
an excellent evergreen fence plant.

It is not only this kind of shrub we may use, for
beautiful climbers, such as the wild species of Clematis,
which are often easily raised from seed ; or small
plants may be got for a few pence from English
or continental nurseries. I speak of such kinds as
the Virgin's Bower (C. Viticella), C. Flammula, C. montana, C. graveolens, C. campanulata and other wild
kinds, many of them yet to be introduced. The
gardeners are not always alive to their charms, and
if we get them at all, we may sometimes have to put
them in newly-made fences, in which they do and
look well. The large Bindweed and other climbers
may also be used in these free fences. Our common
Ivy is a delightful plant in fences, and some of the

less common and more graceful kinds (when plentiful in gardens) may be used. The same is true of many hardy climbers. It is not only shrubs and climbers we may add to our fences, but hardy flowers of the more vigorous kinds, which indeed often thrive well in hedge banks. I have planted in them bulbs of Narcissus, Tulip, Violets, Wild Strawberries, Star-worts, Moon Daisies, and various vigorous plants which grow perhaps too well in the garden. They do not add to the strength of the fence, but when large rough fences are made they often adorn it, whereas the shrubs above mentioned, Wild Roses and Briers, tie the fence together, and add security as well to its beauty.

In certain parts of Kent, on the hills, we see a very picturesque fence, of unclipped Yew, creeping in dark single files across the hills, here and there bearing garlands of wild Clematis. A fence suggested by this may often be useful in gardens, and be improved upon. I mean an unclipped fence of native Evergreens, not planted close, and among them, at intervals, flowering shrubs. Where Yew is used for this, such a fence should not be put in open fields, but in country places there is often occasion for such a free dividing line, to separate orchards and other enclosures from roads or woods. Such a fence I made to protect the west side of the new orchard at Gravetye, running from the moat up the hill, using Yew in this case, as there was no grazing on either side; between the Yews were planted Medlar, Sloe, Quince, Wild Rose, Sweet Brier, Wild Raspberry, and, here and there, Virgin's Bower and other Clematises, and the large Bindweed, which could do no harm there. This fence is meant to be a good shelter as well as a division, and such fences should not be clipped if their shelter is to be thought of. They are also much more beautiful unclipped, and where planted on the cold sides of orchards or fields are valuable for the warmth and shelter they give. The Holly in such positions, carrying garlands of Wild Rose, is very beautiful.

CHAPTER VII.

CLIMBERS FOR TREES AND BUSHES.

THE numerous hardy climbers are rarely seen to advantage, owing to their being stiffly trained against walls, and many of them have gone out of cultivation for this reason. One of the happiest ways of enjoying them is that of training them in free ways over trees; in this way many beautiful effects may be secured. In some low trees a graceful creeper may garland their heads; in tall ones the stem only. Some vigorous climbers in time ascend tall trees, and there are few more beautiful than a veil of Clematis montana over a tall tree. Many lovely kinds may be grown, apart from the popular climbers, and there are graceful wild Clematises which have never come into gardens. The same may be said of the Honeysuckles, wild Vines, and various other families. Much of the northern

tree world is garlanded with creepers, which we may
grow in similar ways, and also on rough banks and
in hedgerows.   The trees in our pleasure grounds,
however, have the first claim.

LARGE WHITE CLEMATIS ON YEW TREE AT GREAT TEW.   (C. montana grandiflora.)

Some time ago I saw a Weeping Willow, on the
margin of a lake, its trunk clothed with Virginian
Creeper, and the effect in autumn, when the sun
shone through the drooping branches of the Willow

—whose leaves were just becoming tinged with gold—
upon the crimson of the creeper-covered trunk was
very fine. The Hop is a very effective plant for draping
trees, but the shoots should be thinned out in spring
and not more than three or four allowed to climb
up to the tree. When the leader emerges from the
top of the bush, and throws its long, graceful wreaths
of Hops over the dark green foliage, the contrast is
most effective. The Wistaria is a host in itself, and
should be freely planted against Pines and other
trees, also by itself on banks and in the open ; its
use on houses is too limited for the noblest of hardy
flowering climbers. I have planted many against
Pines and other trees in plantations.

A correspondent, who has added largely to the
charms of a place in Suffolk by means of the wild
garden, writes as follows :—

'Some time ago I discovered and had removed from
the woods to the pleasure grounds a robust Holly, which
had been taken entire possession of by a wild Honeysuckle, which, originating at the root of the tree, had
scrambled up through the branches to the top, and there,
extending itself in all directions, had formed a large head
and hung in festoons all round. The Holly had endured
the subjection for many years, and still seemed to put forth
sufficient shoots and leaves annually to ensure a steady
support to its companion.'

The Honeysuckle in question is an example of
what might be done with such handsome climbers.

The climbing Honeysuckles are now as numerous as delightful, and require very little encouragement to garland a plantation, and flourish in hedgerow or on bank without care.

Mr. Hovey, in a letter from Boston, Mass., wrote me as follows, on certain interesting aspects of tree drapery :—

' Some years ago we planted three or four rows of climbers in nursery rows, about 100 feet long; these consisted of the Virginian Creeper, the Moonseed (Menispermum), Periploca græca, and Celastrus scandens; subsequently, it happened that four rows of Arborvitæs were planted on one side, and

CLIMBING SHRUB (CELASTRUS), ISOLATED ON THE GRASS; way of growing woody Climbers away from walls or other supports.

about the same number of rows of Smoke trees, Philadelphus, and Dogwood (Cornus florida) on the other. For three or four years many of these climbers were taken up annually until rather too old to remove, and year by year the Arbor-vitæs and shrubs were thinned until what were too large to transplant remained. The land was not wanted then, and the few scattered trees and climbers grew on until the climbers had fairly taken possession of the trees, and they are now too beautiful to disturb! Some of the Arbor-vitæ are overrun with the Moonseed (Menispermum), whose large leaves overlap one another like slates on a roof. Over others, the leaves of the Periploca scramble, and also the Celastrus, and on still others the deep green leaves of the Ampelopsis completely festoon the tree; from among the tops of the Sumach the feathery tendrils of the Ampelopsis, and, just now, its deep blue berries, hold full sway. The Apios tuberosa is indigenous, and springs up everywhere as soon as our land is neglected. This also has overrun several trees, and coils up and wreathes each outstretching branch with its little bunches of fragrant brownish flowers. One Hemlock Spruce has every branch loaded with the Apios and profuse with blossoms. When such strong climbers as Bignonia and Wistaria take possession of a shrub they generally injure it; but the very slender stems of Menispermum and Apios die entirely to the ground after the first sharp frost, and the slender stems of the others do not appear to arrest the growth of the Arbor-vitæ.'

But the noblest kind of climbers forming drapery for trees are not so often seen as some of the general favourites mentioned above. A neglected group are the wild Vines, plants of the highest beauty, which, if allowed to spring through the tall trees, which they would quickly do, would soon charm by their bold grace. With these might be associated certain free growing species of Ampelopsis. In the garden of MM. Van Eden, at Haarlem, I was surprised to see a Liane, in the shape of Aristolochia Sipho

or Dutch-
man's Pipe,
which had
grown high
into a fine
old decid-
uous Cy-
press. When
I saw it early
in spring the
leaves had
not appear-
ed on either
the tree or
its compan-
ion, and
the effect of
the old rope-
like stems
was very
picturesque.
The Aristo-
lochia as-
cends to a
height of
over thirty-
five feet on
the tree,
which was a
superb one.

A LIANE IN THE NORTH. Aristolochia and Deciduous Cypress.

WOODLAND WALK (Belvoir).

CHAPTER VIII.

IT must not be thought that the wild garden can be formed only in places where there is some extent of rough pleasure ground. Pretty results may be had from it in even small gardens, on the fringes of shrubberies and plantations, and on open spaces between shrubs, where we may have plant-beauty instead of garden-graveyards—the dug shrubbery borders seen in gardens, public or private. Every shrubbery that is so needlessly dug over every winter may be full of beauty. The custom of digging shrubbery borders prevails now in almost every garden, and there is no worse custom! When winter is once come, almost every gardener, with the best intentions, prepares to make war upon the roots of everything in his shrubbery. The practice is to trim and to mutilate the shrubs and to dig all over the ground that is full of feeding roots. Choice shrubs are disturbed, herbaceous plants are disrooted, bulbs are injured, the roots as well as the tops of shrubs are mutilated, and a miserable aspect is given to the borders; while the only 'improvement' that comes of the process is the darkening of the surface of the upturned earth!

Illustrations of these bad practices are seen by the mile in our London parks in winter. Walk through any of them at that season and observe the borders around masses of shrubs. Instead of finding the earth covered with vegetation close to the margin and each shrub grown into a fair example of its kind, we find a wide expanse of dug ground, and the shrubs upon it with an air of having recently suffered from a whirl-wind, that led to the removal of mutilated branches. Rough pruners go before the diggers and trim in the shrubs for them, so that nothing may be in the way; and then come the diggers, plunging their spades deeply about plants, shrubs or trees. The first shower that occurs after this digging exposes a whole network of torn-up roots. The same thing occurs everywhere —in botanic gardens as well as in our large West-end parks, and year after year the brutal process is repeated.

While such evil practice is the rule, we cannot have a fresh carpet of beautiful living things in a plantation. What secrets one might have in the hidden parts of these now dug shrubberies—in the half-shady spots where little colonies of rare exotic wildings might thrive! All the labour that produces these ugly dug borders is worse than thrown away, and the shrubs would even do better if left alone.

If no annual digging is to be done, nobody will grudge a thorough preparation of the ground at first. Then the planting should be so done as to defeat the digger, and this could best be done by covering the whole surface with groups of free-growing hardy plants and of dwarf Evergreens. Happily, there is quite enough of these to be had suitable for every soil. Light, moist, peaty or sandy soils, where such things as the sweet-scented Daphne Cneorum would spread forth its neat bushes, would be better than a stiff soil; but for every soil good plants might be found. The dwarf Evergreen Sun Roses (Helianthemum), Evergreen Candytuft (Iberis), Purple Rock Cress (Aubrietia), Arabis, Alyssum, dwarf shrubs, little conifers like the creeping Cedar and the Savin, and Lavender in spreading groups and colonies would help well. All these should spread out into wide groups covering the margin and helping to cut off the stiff line which usually borders a shrubbery, and the margin should be varied also as regards the height of the plants.

In one spot we might have a wide-spreading colony of the prostrate Savin bush with graceful evergreen branchlets; in another the dwarf Cotoneasters might form the front, relieved in their turn by Scotch or pretty Wild Roses of dwarf stature; and herbs, dwarf evergreen or grey shrubs, and stout herbaceous plants, in colonies between the trees.

*In forming a garden plantation of evergreen or other
trees, the best way is not to plant in the far too thickly set
way that is usual, but rather openly, and then cover all the
space between the trees with groups of easily increased
hardy flowers.* This was done at Gravetye, in the belt
of evergreen trees I planted west of the house, using
among other plants Compass plants, Starworts (Aster),
Lavender, Moon Daisies, Geraniums (hardy spreading
kinds), Jerusalem Sage (Phlomis), Fuchsia, scarlet
Bee Balm (Monarda), Evening Primrose, Sea Lyme
Grass (Elymus), Alum root (Heuchera), Stenactis
speciosa, Prairie Sunflowers, Rheum Emodi, Globe
Thistle, and Golden Yarrow. The effects were the best
we had, the plants giving little trouble after planting,
but, on the other hand, saving us trouble. Before
we planted in this way weeds were a constant trouble,
but the vigorous colonies of plants wanted all the
good of the ground for themselves, and took care of
the weeds for us! Certainly it was very much less
trouble than an ordinary mixed border ; there was
no staking of any kind, and the stems were not cut
down till late in spring ; they looked very pretty in
colour in winter. This, like every other plan, must
be changed in the course of years ; when the trees
meet there will be less need of the plants, but it is
a system that can be easily suited to the circumstances
as they arise.

All that the well-covered shrubbery would require
would be an occasional weeding or thinning, and in

the case of the choicer plants, a little top-dressing
with fine soil. In suitable soils such dwarf plants
as Forget-me-nots, Violets and Primroses might be
scattered, so as to give the borders interest even at
the dullest seasons; but in large and new plantations
and shrubberies *the best plants are those that give bold
effects and are very hard to kill.*

In beds of choice shrubs, the same plan on a small
scale will do, but in this case rare plants might often
be planted, and that is flower gardening. But the
theme of this book is the planting of things that will
take care of themselves once fairly started, and we
only come into the shrubberies to save them from
ugliness and dreariness by a modification of the same
plan, which to succeed must be done in a bold and
simple way. To do it well, one should have a few
nursery beds of hardy flowers, or frequently divide
and make groups of those that grow and increase
rapidly. The rule should be—never show the naked
earth : clothe it. It need hardly be said that this
argument against digging applies to two or three
beds of shrubs and to places where the 'shrubbery'
is little larger than the dining-room, as much as to
the large country seat, public park and botanic
garden.

One of the prettiest plant pictures I have ever seen
was in a shrubbery forming a belt round a botanic
garden. In the inner and hidden parts, probably
from want of labour, the digging had not been done

for years. Some roots of the common Myrrh (Myrrhis
odorata), thrown out of the garden in digging, had
rooted by accident and spread into a little colony.
Among the tufts of Myrrh some tall white Harebells
came, also thrown out of the flower-beds in the garden
to get rid of them, and the effect of these, standing
above the spreading foliage of the Myrrh in the shade

A BEAUTIFUL ACCIDENT.—A colony of Myrrhis odorata, in shrubbery not dug,
with white Harebells here and there.

of the trees, was very beautiful. The front of the
shrubbery in which this picture was found was as
stiff and hideous as usual—raw earth, full of mutilated
roots, and shrubs cut in for the convenience and the
taste of the diggers. This was in the shrubbery
surrounding the Botanic Garden at Cambridge, where
Mr. Parsons made a sketch of it here engraved on
wood.

There are some advantages, too, in leaving the leaves to nourish the ground and protect it. Here is a note from a friend inquiring about what he thinks difficulties, and an answer to it:—

'You draw a pretty picture of what a shrubbery border should be and how it should be kept in winter. There should be no digging, and the fallen leaves should be left. I fully agree, except as to the leaves. Theoretically, it seems quite right to allow the leaves to lie and decay amidst the surrounding plants, but in practice it does not answer. There are, for instance, in most gardens such things as slugs and snails. These delight in a leafy covering, and, protected from frost by the shelter, will prey upon the perennial green leafage and the starting crowns of the herbaceous plants, and do an immense amount of mischief. Then there are usually in gardens in winter, especially in hard weather, blackbirds and thrushes, which in their efforts to obtain food set all notions of tidiness at defiance. The first storm that came would whirl the disturbed leaves all over the place.'

How do the swarming plants of the woods and copses of the world exist in spite of the slugs? In the garden we may please ourselves as to leaves, and besides all gardens are frequently enriched by soil and other things, but not one leaf would I ever allow to be removed from a clump of shrubs or trees on lawn or pleasure ground, and I should prefer the leaves all over the place to dug borders. In a plantation of choice trees, their branches resting on the ground, with low shrubs and hardy plants like, say, Starworts between, there are impediments to the leaves rushing about in the way mentioned. Our annual digging, mutilation, raking away of leaves, and exposing on bare earthy borders plants that in Nature shelter each other, and are shielded from hard frost and heat by layers of fallen leaves, which gradually sink into light soil for the young roots, are practices that must be given up by all who look into the needs of our hardy garden flora. In my plantation 10,000 stems of Starworts and other plants all the winter standing brown in their place, keep hold of all the leaves that may get among them!

Woods.

Woods vary so much in their character and the plants growing beneath the trees, that we may for ever see different effects, and a thousand things may be suggested to us by woods. In Pine woods in mountain districts we may see sheets of Ferns and even alpine flowers in them, and our own southern Pine woods in Surrey and Hants often spring out of gardens of lovely Heaths. In the same parish we find woods so close with oaks and underwood, that only tall and stout flowers like wood Angelica, showy Ragwort, large wood Grasses and Foxglove, French Willow and Bracken will grow—these, too, if one goes into the wood and looks at them, often giving us pictures. But this little book cannot tell us the lessons to be learnt about flowers in the woods of the world, whether in those set out by man for his use, or in the great and more stately woods of the earth mother, as, say, in those of the mountains of California, a garden woodland with lovely Evergreens set below great Pine trees, and on the ground lace-work of delicate Ferns and a thousand flowers.

Here is a letter from an observer of what goes on in the woods of New England.

'I go into the woods in the spring-time, and find them carpeted with Dog's-tooth Violets, Wood Anemones, blue and purple Hepaticas, Spring Beauty, Trillium, Blood-root, Star-flowers, Solomon's Seal, Gold Thread, trailing Arbutus, and a host of pretty little flowers, all bright, arising from their bed of decaying grass and tree leaves, and many of them in perfection, too, before a tree has spread a leaf; nourished and sheltered by their tree friends. When their petals drop and their leaves are mature, the trees expand their leafy canopy and save the little nurslings from a scorching sun. And early as the earliest, too, the out-skirts of the woods and meadows are painted blue and white with hosts of Violets and speckled everywhere with Bluets, or little Innocents, as the children call them. Woodsias, tiny Aspleniums, and other Ferns are unfolding their fronds along the chinks among the stones; the common Polypody is reaching over blocks and boulders, and even the exposed rocks, with their rough and Lichen-bearded faces, are beautiful. Every nook and cranny among them, and every little mat of earth upon them, is chequered with the flowery print of the Canada Columbine, the Virginia

Saxifrage, and the grey Corydalis. What can be prettier than the Partridge Berry (Mitchella repens), the Twin-flower (Linnæa borealis)—does well with us – Creeping Winter Green (Gaultheria procumbens), Bearberry (Arctos-taphylos Uva-Ursi), Cowberry (Vaccinium Vitis-idæa), dwarf Cornel (Cornus canadensis), Fringed Polygala (P. paucifolia), the common Pipsissewa (Chimaphila umbellata), with its shining deep green leaves, the Spotted Pipsissewa (C. maculata), the sombre-hued Pyrola and Galax, and that bright Club Moss (Lycopodium lucidulum)?

' One day last spring, when strolling through the Medford Wood, I came upon an open meadow with a high bank— cleared timber land—on one side. Adown this bank in a rocky bed came a little stream of water, bordered on both sides with patches of Blood-root, with large blossoms, clasped erect in their own leaf-vases and sparkling in the sun, while the sward and other vegetation around were yet dormant. True, near by in the hollow, the malodorous Skunk Cabbage was rank in leaf and flower, and the Indian Poke was rushing out its plaited, broadly oval leaves, and away in the streamlet a few Marsh Marigolds glittered on the water. But the Blood-root is neither an aquatic nor a bog plant, but most at home in the leaf-mould beds of rich woodlands.

' Hereabouts, a little wild flower (Erythronium americanum), more commonly known as Dog's-tooth Violet, is a charming plant, with variegated handsome leaves and comely flowers in earliest spring. In low copses, in rich deposits of vegetable mould, it grows around here in the utmost profusion. In one place by the side of a wood is a sort of ditch, which is filled with water in winter, but is dry in summer, wherein is collected a mass of leaf-soil. Here the Yellow Dog's-tooth

Violet runs riot, and forms the densest kind of matted sod, all bespeckled with yellow blossoms before a tree has spread a leaf. When Blackberry bushes get a growing and sprawling everywhere, the trees expand their leafy shade, and grass and weeds grow up and cover the surface of the earth, it is all too late for evil, the early flower's mission for a year is ended ; it has blossomed and retired.'— W. FALCONER.

THE WOOD WILD GARDEN.

Longleat is one of the first places in which the idea of the wild garden in English woods was ably carried out by the late forester, Mr. Berry. With such a fine variety of surface and soil, the place offers many positions in which the plants of other countries as cold as our own could be so planted that they would take care of themselves in the woods. A forester's duties make it difficult for him to carry out such an idea, and even to know the plants that are likely to succeed is in itself a knowledge which every planter does not possess ; however, the idea was clearly understood and carried out well, so far as possible in the face of rabbits, which are the great destroyers of almost all ground vegetation. To get the necessary quantities of plants, a little nursery in which could be raised numbers of the more vigorous perennials, bulbs and climbers was required. If the *Wild Garden* is to be carried out on the old dotting principle of the herbaceous border, its charming effects cannot be realized. To do it rightly we must group and mass as Nature does. Though we may enjoy a single flower or tuft here and there, the true way is to make pretty colonies of plants, one or two kinds prevailing in a spot; in that way we may secure distinct effects in each place, and better means of meeting the wants of a plant, inasmuch as dealing with a colony we can easily see the result of putting the plants in any soil or place. Among the plants used are vigorous hardy climbers on old trees, Thorn and other bushes of little value—Japanese and other Honeysuckles, Virginian creepers, Clematis, Wistarias and others. A part of the arboretum is devoted to these plants, and forms a wild garden, where the Poet's Narcissus may be found among Sweet Briers, Lilacs and many kinds of fragrant shrubs and stout perennials. While carrying out wild gardening, pure and simple—that is to say, the naturalization of foreign hardy plants—beautiful native kinds were also planted when not naturally wild in the neighbourhood. Thus the Lily of the Valley has been brought in quantities and planted wide along the drives, and so have the Meadow Saffrons and the Snowflakes and Daffodils. To group and scatter these in a natural and pretty way has required care, the tendency of the men being, almost in spite of themselves, to plant in stiff and set or too regular masses.

Few things are more delightful to anybody who

cares about hardy plants than naturalizing the Lily
of the Valley in woody places about a country house. It
is in every garden, and very often so crowded and so
starved that it seldom flowers well. A bare garden
border is not so suitable for it as a thin wood or little
openings in a copse, where it enjoys enough light. And
by planting it in various positions and soils, we may
secure an important difference as to bloom. On a cool

THE LILY OF THE VALLEY IN COPSE.

northern slope it blooms ten days later than on a warm
garden border. Recently different varieties of Lily
of the Valley have been collected, and are cultivated.
This fact should be noted by any who would, in places
where the Lily of the Valley does not grow wild, desire
to establish it.

There are advantages in plantation culture for many
hardy plants — the shelter, shade, and soil affording
for some things conditions more suitable than garden

borders. The warmth of the wood, too, is an advantage, and the fallen leaves help to protect the plants in all ways. In a hot country, plants that love cool places could be grown in a wood, while they would perish if exposed. Mr. G. F. Wilson has made himself a remarkably interesting wild garden in a wood, from which he sent me in the autumn of 1880 flowering stems of the American Swamp Lily (L. superbum) 11 feet high. These Lilies grow in a woody bottom where rich dark soil has gathered, and where there is shelter and shade.

Mr. Wilson sends me (August, 1893) a list of the things that did best in his wood wild garden. Lilium auratum (many thousands), and some of its varieties such as platyphyllum and rubro-vittatum; Lilium superbum (many), L. pardalinum and varieties, L. Szovitzianum, L. giganteum, L. cordifolium, Leichtlinii, and others in smaller quantities. Iris Kæmpferi, raised in most part from seed, in different parts of the garden from 5000 to 6000 clumps, Iris sibirica and orientalis in large quantities, and other Irises in smaller numbers. Most of the plants liking heath soil such as heaths Andromeda, Ledum, Gaultheria procumbens, Linnæa borealis, Pyrola, Shortia galacifolia, Galax aphylla, Xerophyllum asphodeloides, Gentians — Gentianella, G. septemfida in large quantities, G. asclepiadea blue and white, hundreds of clumps, a number of other Gentians in smaller quantities, and many Hypericums. 'Rhododendrons grow so freely in our wood that we planted an acre with seedlings which were crowding their parents.'

'Though the wood comprises but a few acres, there is a wide range of soil and aspect in it. The wood is chiefly of Oaks; beneath them is a great depth of leaf soil—a soil in which many plants will thrive if the exposure is right for them. A better place for shade-loving plants could not well be found. Outside the wood is a wide stretch of sloping treeless ground fully exposed, consisting of a good loam, and between it and the wood is a low-lying portion through which runs a little stream; in another place is a deep bog where one might sink knee-deep in soft mud, and where Calthas and such plants thrive.

'Lilies abound everywhere in the wood, and may be counted by the thousand under various conditions of soil and aspect. For Lilium auratum, total shade is worse than full exposure, particularly if the season be a wet one. The healthiest plants are well sheltered and have a partial shade. Here North American Lilies of the superbum and pardalinum types may be seen probably finer than in their native haunts. The tall stems of the Swamp Lily rise up midst brushwood and carry huge heads of flowers that make the slender stems bow with every breath of wind. Never till now had we seen large colonies of Lilies of the dahuricum and elegans type, the effect of which was charming. Just at the bottom of the slope, in a deep loam, where they were fully exposed, they were the finest, some of the stems being 4 feet and 5 feet high, and loaded with blossoms. Higher up were masses of Lilium monadelphum and its varieties, called severally Szovitzianum, Loddigesianum, and colchicum, all uncommonly fine, the stems tall and stout, and carrying huge heads of flowers. In this spot the soil is a deep loam, neither too light nor too heavy, but of such a character as just to suit this Lily as well as all the Martagons, the old white L. candidum, testaceum, and, in fact, all the European kinds.

'Besides Lilies may be noticed here—other interesting results—gigantic tufts of Funkias in the shadiest part of the wood, for, as a rule, they like sun. It is clear they are not fastidious in this respect, for finer tufts we have not seen; those who would relieve the monotony of woodland walks might plant by the margins tufts of F. Sieboldi, F. ovata and F. subcordata, avoiding the small-growing kinds, especially those with variegated foliage. One of the greatest successes has been with the charming little Epigæa repens or May Flower of the N. American woods. Here it forms quite a carpet, amidst the fallen leaves, and under these conditions pretty Linnæa borealis also grows.'—*Garden*.

A great many beautiful plants haunt the woods, we cannot change their nature easily: and even if we grow them well in open places, their bloom will not be so enduring as in the wood. The secret of wild gardening is adapting plants to the soil. The Solomon's Seal is typical of certain wild garden plants that do not go off early, like Daffodils and Crocus, and therefore require a different position—the friendly shelter of wood or copse. In my district there was not a bit of it wild, and it was important to secure so beautiful a thing in large groups, without giving any of the flower garden to it—I mean places where we wanted to grow our Roses and Carnations, and the many things on which the beauty of the flower-garden depends throughout our summer. So I put it pretty freely under a plantation of Hollies, right out of the garden, in a place never disturbed, and there it takes care of itself, and flowers abundantly without any kind of attention. A prettier thing could hardly be seen in masses. At about the same time roots of it were scattered in the Moat shaw where there were large oaks overhead, and the usual underwood. They have done pretty well every year since, but each year they get stronger, and this year we have been surprised at their beauty, especially in the lower and richer parts of the copse, where they found a depth of washed-down soil near a small stream. It is delightful to creep through the undergrowth and see their beautiful forms a yard high or more fully blown and very much prettier than in a mass in the pleasure garden, because they grow separately, and one gets the full value of the arching and bell-laden stem growing out of sheets of Bluebells. No manure or attention has even been given beyond planting—taking a basket of roots, making a few holes in the copse here and there at not too regular intervals and letting the plants alone ever since. In districts where Solomon's Seal grows in the woods there is no need to plant it, but there are many places where it does not; and where there are no woods it is sure to make a charming feature in the shrubbery. I remember, at Angers, seeing some forms of it tall, and natives of central France—at least, I was told so by M. Boreau, the then director of the Angers garden. There is also a tall American kind, which would be very charming if naturalized in similar places. In the same wood with Solomon's Seal I have also been planting Narcissus Stella, which naturalized in this way, and blooming at the same time, has made the pretty copse a charming spring garden. Solomon's Seal in masses shows good colour of the leaves in autumn.

In the hot days of May, 1893, in walking from Compiègne to Pierrefonds, in the Forest of Compiègne, we passed by many acres of Lily of the Valley in bloom under trees. It was one of the few things that retained its delightful freshness in the greatest drought within living memory. As people so often ask for plants suitable for growing in bare places under trees, they might try the Lily of the Valley. It is so common in gardens, and gets so thick when planted in rich ground, that many can spare some for trial. It is a mistake to suppose that it requires rich ground. The attempt to grow Grass in shady and half-shady places is often a failure, and it is well to know of some plants that will grow in such situations. The Lily of the Valley is one of the things that will form a carpet and require no attention. It would be pretty to vary its mass here and there with groups of hardy Ferns, Solomon's Seal, and Woodruff.

Colonies of POET'S NARCISSUS and BROAD LEAVED SAXIFRAGE.

CHAPTER IX.

WOODLAND DRIVES AND GRASS WALKS.

In the larger country places the often noble opportunities for beautiful woodland drives are not always
seized, sometimes because people have the primitive
and wholly inartistic idea that the proper way to make
a drive is to plant two or four lines of trees along it.
These are often set far too close, and as they are
rarely thinned in time, the whole ends in a gloomy
tunnel without air, light, or shade. Even where the
avenue is not the 'leading feature,' drives through
woods and parks are too narrow.

Fine airy effects might be got by breadths of low
covert or fern beside drives, and these drives should
take the line of easiest grade, and the best for views
where possible. There is no reason why drives should
not pass under trees here and there, but, generally,
a better effect is got by keeping the groups and fine
trees a little off the drive, and having bold groups of

hardy shrubs and carpets of plants as a foreground to the woodland picture.

Here and there, as at Penrhyn, are some beautiful glades of wild Fern coming near the drives, and there is a lovely example at Powys of what our native plants do in the foreground of a really picturesque drive. But by a little forethought we may easily get finer things in this way from Thorns, Foxglove, or Willow herb, wide sheets of large Ferns with breaks of Wild Roses, large rambling colonies of Sweet Brier, lovely fields of native Heaths, double Furze as well as the single kind, Broom on poor banks and Partridge Berry in half-shady places—a host of beautiful things that would spread about and give excellent covert as well as pretty effects.

Of regularly formed roads—those made of gravel, flint, or other stone—there are three times too many in most country seats. It is wise economy to reduce these to the real needs of the place. All places are the uglier for being beset with gate lodges, which are usually ugly in themselves and lead to needless cutting up of beautiful ground, the increase of gates, and the springing up of the iron fiend in every direction. As the artistic and true way is to reduce as much as possible these needless drives often made for mere show, or to save five minutes, let those we keep be as good in grade and view as we can make them, and have as many picturesque charms as we may give them.

We never have enough of Grass walks and drives.

When we want a way merely for our own convenience, by far the best is a Grass drive or walk through pretty woodland scenery, over park, hill, or by stream or river. A delightful privilege which English gardens have, more than others, is that of having Grass walks of the finest texture and verdure. At Holwood, in the late Lord Derby's time, it was pleasant to see the number and the delightful charm of the Grass walks there. Around our houses we must have good firm walks; but once free of the house and regular gardens, one may break into the graceful Grass walks without injury to anything. Some prefer gravel walks in winter, but the gravel walk is not always much drier than a well-made Grass walk; however, as we use our gardens most in summer, it does not matter so much. Even on heavy soils Grass walks may be delightful the greater part of the year, and on dry soils we need not fear the wet.

It is not only the effect of Grass walks that is in their favour—they are a great economy. They can be cleaned with one-fourth of the labour which the gravel walks take. Once free of the garden, it is rather in the rougher parts of the pleasure ground and about the park that Grass walks are made with the best results. The line of ground should be studied both for ease in walking and mowing, and for the sake of the best views. Nothing in gardening rewards us so well as well-thought-out Grass walks and drives. If, as they should be, the gravel walks about the house are reduced to the strictly necessary dimensions, it is surprising how much the wearisome trouble of hoeing is done away with. The toilsome labour of ripping up walks, raking, and hoeing, seen in so many gardens, need not, happily, go on. It only makes matters worse by softening the walks, for the hoeing is a serious labour in the hot days and is absolutely unnecessary.

Having our Grass drive or Grass walk, what shall we place beside it? Our British plants are as fair as any others, and we may see as beautiful groups of fern, heather, thorn, and bramble as are given by the flora of any country. Still, those who care for the plants of other countries have by the Grass walk a charming opportunity of adding other pretty things to our own wild flowers.

There is much difference in districts as to their wild flowers and the effects from native plants. Some places may be full of beautiful things—others have very few. What a place has in this way depends upon the cultivation and the quality of the land, and other conditions which need not be gone into; it is enough to know that these differences exist. Where the natural vegetation is poor, there is all the greater need for adding beautiful things of easy naturalization. Our wood anemone is pretty in the fields and groves in spring, but the blue Apennine anemone, which is quite hardy, gives us a wholly distinct and charming colour, and this is true of other things. The high mountain plants of the Alps of Europe, to whose flora many early flowers belong, give us the precious gift of earliness ; crocus, narcissus, and scilla, all come before our own early flowers awake, while nearly all are as hardy as our own native flowers. Then there are many hardy climbers which, if we planted them among trees, would be quite as beautiful as any native climbers, of which the number is too small. The Indian Mountain Clematis is hardy, and as easy to establish as our native Clematis, while it is more beautiful, and there are other beautiful plants one may add to our own, though, generally, it will be safer to trust to our native flora by drives. The prettiest brake of shrubs I ever saw was an immense group of the common Barberry at Compton Winyates, laden with berries weeping down with glowing colour.

Much may be done in the direction of Grass walks to take them not only where the views and landscape charm us, but also where the native flora shows itself best. Very often our common ferns in the west country and in moist districts make themselves great ferneries which ought to be seen. The idea that the fernery can only be made with heaps of old stone or other rubbish is too absurd to be worth disputing. The plants rarely grow naturally in that way, and the most vigorous and effective of ferns, which make evergreen covert and give such cool and beautiful effects, certainly do not. There are also numbers of fine hardy North American and other ferns tempting us to naturalize them, but for all artistic ends our native ferns are sufficient.

Still those who have ever seen the fine North
American hardy ferns in their own country, sometimes
in more severe climates than that of our own country,
will often be tempted to naturalize the more vigorous
kinds—success in which will depend on the positions
chosen for them.

CHAPTER X.

THE BROOK-SIDE, WATER AND BOG GARDENS.

SOLOMON'S SEAL AND HERB PARIS, in copse by streamlet.

In the water, at least, plants do not trouble us for attention. If we take the trouble to establish them the rest is easy, and therefore those living near lake or stream may find much interest in adorning them with beautiful flower life of our own and other lands. The richness of our own country in handsome water-plants is not known to many even of those who know our wild flowers —until perhaps they row up a back-water of the Thames, where the water-plants are often superb, or see the great size and variety of those by the Norfolk Broads.

Nearly all landscape gardeners seem to have put a higher value on the pond than on the brook as an ornament to the garden; but many pictures might be formed by a brook on its way through glade or meadow. No such beauty comes through the pond, which gives us water in repose—imprisoned water; while the brook ripples between mossy rocks or flower-fringed banks, its margin, too, giving an excellent place for hardy flowers. Hitherto we have only used in such places water or bog plants, but the improvement of the brook-side will be most readily effected by planting the banks also with vigorous hardy flowers, making it a wild garden, in fact. Many of our finest herbaceous plants, from Iris to Meadow-sweet, thrive in the moist soil; many hardy flowers, also, that do not in nature prefer such soil, exist in health in it. Plants on the bank would have this merit over water-plants, that we could fix them, whereas water-plants are apt to spread too much and often one kind exterminates the rest. The plants, of course, should be such as would grow freely among Grass and take care of themselves. If distinct groups were encouraged, the effect would be all the better. The common way of repeating a plant at intervals would spoil all : groups of free hardy things, different in each place, as one passed, would be best ; Day Lilies ; Iris, many ; Gunnera ; Starwort ; American swamp Lilies in peaty soil ;

COLONY OF HARDY EXOTIC FLOWERS, naturalized by brook-side.

the deep rose variety of the Loosestrife ; Golden Rods ; the taller and stouter Bell-flowers (Campanula) ; the Compass plants (Silphium) ; Monkshoods ; the free-flowering Yuccas ; the hardiest flame-flowers (Tritoma) ; the stouter kinds of Yarrow (Achillea) ; the perennial Lupin ; the red and other Meadow-sweets as well as our own wild kind—these are some of many types of hardy flowers which would grow freely near the water-side apart wholly from the plants that naturally frequent the water. With these hardy plants too, a variety of the nobler hardy ferns would thrive, as the Struthiopteris ; and the Royal Fern would also come in well here.

We will now consider the plants that naturally belong to the water. Water-plants of northern and temperate regions add much to the beauty of a garden if well chosen. A great deal of variety may be added to the margins, and here and there to the surface, of water, by means of hardy aquatics. Usually we see the same monotonous vegetation all round the margin if the soil be rich ; in some cases, where the bottom is of gravel, there is little or no vegetation, but an unbroken ugly line of washed earth between wind and water. In others, water-plants thicken till they become an eyesore—not only submerged weeds, but such as the Water Lilies when matted together. A plant or group of plants of the Water Lily, with its fine leaves and flowers, is beautiful ; but when it runs over a piece of water and water-fowl cannot make way through it, then even this fine plant loses its charms. No garden water, however. should be without a few groups of the Water Lily. Where the bottom is not rich enough, earth might be gathered in certain spots for the growth of the Nymphæa, and thus grown it would not spread much. In the summer of 1893,

at Middleton Hall, Tamworth, I saw the finest example
I remember of its beauty, not only in growth and large
flowers, but in effect over a lake—in masses and
sheets divided by open water—an enormous sheet
of Water Lilies, and the picture, in association with
a pretty old manor house, was lovely. The flowers
were very large, and of two forms—one with a bronzy-
green outer division of the flower, and a flush of delicate
pink inside; the other, a smaller form, pure white with
dark green outer divisions; so we have at least two
forms of our native Water Lily, and there may be others.
In the numerous waters which have to be occasionally
cleared of sediment in gardens and parks, instead of
throwing all the mud on to the land, it would be better
to put some of it in masses near the margins of lakes
in which Water Lilies and other vigorous plants might
grow, and from which they would not wander far. It
is one way and the best of keeping rambling water-
plants in groups, instead of spread all over the water.
The Yellow Water Lily (Nuphar lutea), though not so
beautiful as the preceding, is worth a place; then there
is the large N. advena, a native of North America,
which pushes its leaves boldly above the water,
and is bold in habit. The American White Water
Lily (Nymphæa odorata) is a noble species, and there
are other species, while our gardens have lately been
enriched with a series of noble hybrids of these plants,
soft yellow, rose, and of other good colours. When
these are increased the hardiest of them will be good

to add to our water-gardens. A very pretty effect is that of a sheet of Villarsia belting round the margin of a lake near a woody recess, and before it, in deeper water, a group of Water Lilies. The Villarsia is a pretty little water-plant, with Nymphæa leaves and golden flowers, which give a beautiful effect under a bright sun. It is not very common in Britain, though, where found, generally very plentiful.

Not rare—growing, in fact, in nearly all districts of Britain—but beautiful and singular, is the Buckbean or Bog-bean (Menyanthes trifoliata), with flowers fringed on the inside with white filaments, and the round buds blushing on the top with rose. It will grow in a bog or any moist place, in or by the margin of water. For grace, no water-side plant surpasses Equisetum Telmateia, which, in deep soil, in shady places near water, often grows several feet high, the long, close-set, slender branches depending from each whorl in a singularly graceful manner. It will grow on the margins of lakes and streams, especially among water-side bushes, or in boggy spots in the shade, and will run by thousands through the worst and stiffest soil.

As a picturesque plant on the margin of water, few are finer than the Great Water Dock (Rumex Hydrolapathum); its fine leaves of a lurid red in the autumn — a grand 'foliage' plant, and, unlike many water-plants, not spreading much. This plant, like many others named here, needs no care after planting, and thus is a true wild-garden plant. The Cat's-tail (Typha) must not be forgotten: the narrow-leaved one (T. angustifolia) is more graceful than the common one (T. latifolia). Carex pendula is excellent for the margins of water, its elegant drooping spikes being quite distinct in their way. It is common in England, more so than Carex Pseudo-cyperus, which grows well in a foot or two of water or on the margin of a muddy pond. Carex paniculata forms a thick stem, often 3 ft. or 4 ft. high, somewhat like a tree Fern, with luxuriant masses of drooping leaves, and on that account is transferred to moist places in gardens, and cultivated by some,

CYPERUS LONGUS.

though generally these large specimens soon perish. Scirpus lacustris (the Bulrush) is too good a plant to be left out, as its stems, sometimes attaining a height of more than 7 ft. and even 8 ft., look very imposing; and Cyperus longus is also a fine plant, reminding one of the Papyrus when in flower. It is found in some of

the southern counties of England. Poa aquatica
might also be used. Cladium Mariscus is another
distinct water-side plant which is worth a place.

If one chose to name the plants that grow in British
and European waters, a long list might be made, but
plants having no distinct character or no beauty of
flower would be useless; it is only by a selection of the
best plants that gardening of this kind can charm us.

Those who enjoy the flowering Rush (Butomus
umbellatus) in blossom are not likely to omit it now.
It is a native of the greater part of Europe and Asia,
and of the central and southern parts of England
and Ireland. Plant it not far from the margin, and it
likes rich muddy soil. The Arrow-head (Sagittaria),
frequent in England and Ireland, but not in Scotland,
might be associated with this; and there is a finer
double exotic kind, which is really a handsome plant,
its flowers resembling, but larger than, those of the
old white Double Rocket. This used to be grown
in abundance in the pleasure gardens at Rye House,
Broxbourne, where it filled a wide ditch, and was
very handsome in flower. It forms large egg-shaped
tubers, and in searching for these, ducks destroy the
plants occasionally. Calla palustris is a beautiful bog-
plant, and nothing gives a better effect creeping over
rich, soft, boggy ground. It will also grow by the
side of water. Calla æthiopica (the beautiful Lily of
the Nile) is hardy in the south if planted rather deep.
Pontederia cordata is a stout and hardy water-herb,

with erect habit, and blue flowers. The Sweet-flag will be associated with the Water Iris (I. Pseudacorus), and a number of exotic Irises will thrive in wet ground, such as I. sibirica, ochroleuca, graminea, and others. The Cape Pond Flower (Aponogeton distachyon) is a native of the Cape of Good Hope, a singularly pretty plant, which is hardy in our climate, and, from its sweetness and curious beauty, a good plant to have. It frequently succeeds in water not choked by weeds,

THE CAPE POND WEED in an English ditch in winter.

and wherever there are springs that tend to keep the water a little warmer than usual it seems to thrive in any part of the country. The Water Ranunculuses, which sheet over our pools in spring and early summer with such silvery beauty, are not worth an attempt at cultivation, so rambling are they; and the same applies to not a few other things of interest. As beautiful as any plant is the Water Violet (Hottonia palustris). It occurs most frequently in the eastern and central districts of England and Ireland, and is charming in ditches. A companion for the Marsh Marigold (Caltha) and its varieties is the very large and showy Ranunculus Lingua, which grows in rich ground to a height of 3 feet or more.

If with our water-garden we combine the wild-garden herbaceous plants—I mean the handsomer of the hardy flowers that love moist or heavy soil — some of the loveliest effects in gardens will be ours. The margins of lakes and streams are happily not upturned by the spade in winter; and hereabouts, just away from the water-line, many a vigorous and hardy flower (among the thousands now in our gardens) may be grown and will afterwards take care of itself. The Globe flowers form

DAY LILY by margin of water.

beautiful effects in such positions, and would endure as long as the Grass. Near the various Irises that love the water-side might be planted those that thrive in moist ground. The singular Californian Saxifraga peltata is a noble plant for the water-side. It would

require a very long list to enumerate all the plants
that would grow near the margins of water, apart
from the true water-plants ; given a strip of ground
beside a stream or lake, a garden of the most delightful
kind may be formed of them. The juxtaposition of
plants inhabiting different situations—water-plants,
water-side plants, and land-plants thriving in moist
ground—would prevent what would, in many cases,
be so undesirable—a general admixture of the whole,

MARSH MARIGOLD AND IRIS in early spring. (See p. 111.)

and greatly add to the effect, which is very fine indeed
where both the surface of the water and the banks are
gay with flowers.

An interesting point in favour of the wild garden *is
the succession of effects* which it may afford, and which
are shown by the illustrations on these pages, both
showing a succession of life on the same spot of
ground.

The bog garden is a home for the numerous children
of the wild that will not thrive on our harsh, bare, and
dry garden borders, but must be cushioned on moss, or

grown in moist peat soil. Many beautiful plants, like the Wind Gentian and Creeping Harebell, grow on our own bogs and marshes, much as these are now encroached upon. But even those who see the beauty of the plants of our own bogs have, as a rule, but a feeble notion of the multitude of charming plants, natives of northern and temperate countries, whose home is the open marsh or the boggy wood. In our own country,

The same spot as in opposite sketch, with aftergrowth of Iris, Meadow-sweet, and Bindweed. (See p. 110.)

we have been so long encroaching upon the bogs that some of us come to regard these as exceptional tracts all over the world. But in new countries in northern climes, one soon learns what a vast extent of the world's surface was at one time covered with bogs. In North America day after day, even from the railroads, one sees the vivid spikes of the Cardinal-flower springing from the wet peaty hollows. Far under the shady woods stretch the black bog-pools, the ground between being so shaky that you move a few steps with difficulty.

One wonders how the trees exist with their roots in such a bath. And where the forest vegetation disappears the American Pitcher-plant (Sarracenia), Golden Club (Orontium), Water Arum (Calla palustris), and a host of other handsome and interesting bog-plants cover the ground for hundreds of acres, with perhaps an occasional slender bush of the swamp Magnolia (M. glauca) among them. In some parts of Canada, where the painfully straight roads are often made through woody swamps, and where the few poor 'houses' offer little to cheer the traveller, he will, if a lover of plants, find con-servatories of beauty in the ditches and pools of dark water beside the roads, fringed with a profusion of stately ferns, and often filled with masses of the pretty Arrow-head.

Southwards and seawards, the bog-flowers become tropical in size and brilliancy, as in the splendid herbaceous Hibiscus, while far north, and west and south along the mountains, the beautiful Mocassin-flower (Cypripedium spectabile) grows the queen of the peat waste. Then in California, all along the Sierras, there are a number of delicate little annual plants grow-ing in small mountain bogs long after the plains have become quite parched, and flowers have quite gone from them. But who shall tell of the beauty of the flowers of the marsh-lands of this globe of ours, from those of the vast bog wastes of America, to those of the breezy uplands of the high Alps, far above the woods, where the mountain bogs teem with Nature's most brilliant flowers, joyous in the sun? No one worthily; for many mountain-swamp regions are as yet as little known to us as those of the Himalaya, with their giant Primroses and many strange flowers. One thing, however, we may gather from our small experiences—that many plants commonly termed 'alpine,' and found on high mountains, are true bog-plants. This must be clear to anyone who has seen our pretty Bird's-eye Primrose in the oozing mountain bogs of Westmoreland, or the Bavarian Gentian in the spongy soil by alpine rivulets, or the Gentianella (Gentiana acaulis) in the snow water.

Bogs are not often found near our gardens nowadays, but, wherever they are, there are many handsome flowers from other countries that will thrive in them as freely as in their native wastes, and among these the strange and beautiful Pitcher Plants of the bogs of North-Eastern America which are hardy here too.

PARTRIDGE BERRY (Gaultheria)

CHAPTER XI.

WILD GARDENING ON WALLS, ROCKS [1], OR RUINS.

ARENARIA BALEARICA, self-planted on wall
at Great Tew.

THERE are hundreds of mountain and rock-plants which thrive better on an old wall, a ruin, a sunk fence, a sloping bank of stone, with earth behind, or a 'dry' wall than they do in the most carefully prepared border! Many an alpine plant, which may have perished in its place in the garden, thrives on an old wall near at hand, as, for example, the pretty Pyrenean Erinus, the silvery Saxifrages of the Alps, Pinks

[1] The rocks meant here are natural ones—not the absurdities too often made in gardens.

like the Cheddar Pink, established on the walls at Oxford, many Stonecrops, Houseleeks, the Purple Rock Cress and Arabis.

In the gardens at Great Tew, in Oxfordshire, the charming Balearic Sandwort, which usually roots over the moist surface of stones, planted itself high up on a wall in a small recess, where half a brick had been displaced. It is suggestive, as so many things are, of the many plants that may be grown on walls.

A mossy old wall, or ruin, gives a home for many rock-plants which no specially-prepared situation

CHEDDAR PINK, SAXIFRAGE, AND FERNS, on cottage wall at Mells, Somerset.

equals; but even on well-preserved walls we can establish rock-plants which year after year will repay us for their planting or sowing. Those who have observed how dwarf plants grow on the mountains, or on stony ground, must have seen in what hard places many flourish, fine tufts sometimes springing from a chink in an arid rock or boulder. They are often stunted in these conditions, but always more enduring than when growing on the ground. Now, numbers of alpine plants perish if planted in the ordinary soil of our gardens, and even do so where much pains are taken to grow them. This results from over-moisture at the root in winter, the plants being made more susceptible of injury by our moist green winters inducing them to make a lingering growth. But by placing many of these fragile plants where their roots have a dry if poor soil they remain in perfect health. Many plants from latitudes a little farther south than our own, and from alpine regions, show on walls and rocks a dwarf, sturdy growth, which enables them to endure a winter quite different from that of their native countries.

In many parts of the country there are few opportunities for this gardening; but in various districts, such as the Wye and other valleys, there are miles of rock and rough wall-surface, where the scattering of a few seeds of Arabis, Aubrietia, Erinus, Acanthus, Saxifraga, Viola, Stonecrops, and Houseleeks, would give rise to a garden of rock blossoms that would need no care from the gardener. Growing such fine alpine plants as the true Saxifraga longifolia of the Pyrenees on the surface of a rough wall is quite easy.

A few seeds of the Cheddar Pink, for example, sown in a mossy or earthy chink, or even covered with a dust of fine soil, would soon take root; and the plant would live for years in a dwarf and perfectly healthful state. The seedling roots vigorously into the chinks, and gets a hold which it rarely relaxes. The names of some of the plants that will grow on walls will be found at the end of this chapter.

In forming dry or rough walls to support banks we may easily plant many kinds of rock-plants so that they will grow well thereon, but that work belongs rather

THE YELLOW FUMITORY (Corydalis lutea) on wall.

to the planting of a rock-garden, whereas the whole aim of this book is to take advantage of surfaces already at hand for us.

Some of the Families of Rock and Alpine Plants for Walls, Rocks, and Ruins in Britain.

Achillea.
Alyssum.
Antirrhinum.
Arabis.
Arenaria.
Aubrietia.
Campanula
(mountain kinds).
Centranthus.
Cheiranthus.

Coronilla.
Corydalis.
Dianthus.
Draba.
Erinus.
Erodium.
Gypsophila.
Helianthemum.
Hutchinsia.
Iberis.

Lychnis (rock and mountain kinds).
Saxifraga.
Sedum.
Sempervivum.
Silene.
Thymus.
Tunica.
Veronica (rock and mountain kinds).

PURPLE ROCK CRESS (Mountains of Greece).

CHAPTER XII.

WILD AND OTHER ROSES IN THE WILD GARDEN.

PEOPLE who shake their heads about naturalizing plants in grass, and say it cannot be done, will hardly say we cannot enjoy the Wild Roses of Europe and Northern Asia in any rough place. These do not want our assistance to trail over the mountains and adorn the river-bed rocks down to the shore. If the soil of the hillside and the stony waste is enough for them, surely the rich fields of lowland England, and its hedgerows, and the good soil which is found near most country houses will nourish Wild Roses as well as the mountains and heaths. Our own Wild Roses—we know what they do in the midlands, the west country and on the hills, but not many have a just idea how many beautiful Wild Roses there are in the world that are as hardy as our Sweet Brier. If at present many Wild Roses cannot be had at nurseries, there are some interesting kinds that can be, and there is scarcely a country of Europe or Asia that one goes into, in which the seeds of beautiful Wild Roses may not be gathered, and they are easy to raise.

It will not do to put Wild Roses in the flower-garden, where we want choice cultivated flowers ; but there are ways in which any Wild Rose we bring or gather might be delightfully used, i. e. in the shrubbery, and in forming fences and also in beds in the rougher parts of pleasure grounds. It is a very common thing to see the sunk fence, which has been made in so many places, without any plant life upon it, though some is needed for marking the drop and to some extent garlanding the brow of the fence. In my own garden, where I made a sunk fence, we planted groups of various Wild Roses from one end to the other—bold running groups 5 to 7 feet wide, and few things have given us so good a return ; they do not grow high, they garland the sunk fence and add to its effect from both sides and give pretty effects of flower and fruit. I use the Sweet Brier, the American Glossy Rose, the Japan Rose, Scotch Rose, Carolina, and the Russian Wild Rose, and any Wild Roses that are plentiful and grow freely, and take care of themselves.

How may we get a slight idea of the riches of the world in Wild Roses ? I thought I had some notion of it myself till I went to Lyons last September (1892) to get Tea Roses for my garden. These roses of garden origin are the loveliest things raised or grown by man : sweet with all the delicate fragrance of the morning air on down or Surrey heath, having the colours of the

H·HYDE

WILD ROSE growing on a Pollard Ash in Orchardleigh Park, Somerset.

cloud, and all that is loveliest in form of bud and bloom. But these precious roses are things of cultivation only. Without the good gardener's spade and knife they would soon become a tangle with less meaning and beauty than the Wild Brier. Their size and beauty are not to be had without good cultivation, and nothing can so well show us the difference between the Wild Garden and the flower-garden than these fairest garden roses and the Wild Roses of the hills, growing in the same place in quite different ways.

Having got my garden roses a friend happened to say that the Wild Yellow Rose, that has given us the Austrian Yellow Rose, was wild in the region, and I bought a flora of the country to see something about its Wild Roses[1]. In it the Wild Roses are grouped as shown below, and the numbers given represent the species in each section. And this, it will be noted, is only in one region of France.

	SECTIONS.	SPECIES.			SECTIONS.	SPECIES.
I.	SYSTYLÆ.	5		VI.	MONTANÆ.	14
II.	GALLICANÆ.	24		VII.	CANINÆ.	46
III.	PIMPINELLIFOLIÆ.	12		VIII.	RUBIGINOSÆ.	33
IV.	ALPINÆ.	9		IX.	TOMENTOSÆ.	24
V.	SABINIÆ.	5		X.	POMIFERÆ.	8

Here in one district of France, exposed to the alp wind and frost, we have nearly two hundred kinds of Wild Rose: it shows how rich the northern world is in rose beauty—at least to all to whom the earth-born

[1] *Etude des Fleurs.* Renfermant la Flora du bassin moyen du Rhone et de la Loire. Par L'Abbé Cariot. Lyon, 1889.

loveliness of the leaf, bud, blossom, and fruit of the Wild Rose is visible. And these roses want no budding, pruning, or learned cultivation of any kind; but let no one suppose I wish them to take the place of our lovely Tea Roses in the flower-garden. There are, at least in my own garden, places for both.

The Rev. H. N. Ellacombe writes as to old garden Roses among bushes:

'I have here a large Box bush, in the centre of which there has been for many years an Ayrshire Rose. The long branches covered with flowers, and resting on the deep green cushion, have a very beautiful effect. Other Roses may be used in the same way. The Musk Rose of Shakespeare and Bacon would be particularly well suited for this, and would climb up to a great height. Rosa scandens or sempervirens, Rosa multiflora, and perhaps some others, might be grown in the same way; and it would be worth while to experiment with other garden forms, such as Aimée Vibert, purple Boursault, &c. If grown against a tree of thin foliage, such as a Robinia, they would grow quicker and flower sooner; but this is not necessary, for even if grown near a thick-foliaged tree they will soon bring their branches to the outside for the light. But besides climbing Roses, there is another way in which Roses may be combined with trees to great advantage, viz. by planting some of the taller-growing bushes in rough grassy places. These would grow from 6 feet to 10 feet high, and would flower well in such a position. For such a purpose the old Dutch Apple Rose (Rosa villosa var. pomifera) would be very suitable, and so would R. cinnamomea, R. fraxinifolia, R. gallica, R. rubifolia, and the common monthly China.'

WHITE CLIMBING ROSE scrambling over old Catalpa Tree.

Mr. Greenwood Pim writes, referring to the above note :—

' I have two large Hawthorns—round-headed standards— growing close together, so that their edges touch, forming, as it were, two gentle hills with a valley between, and sloping down to within about 6 feet of the lawn. Of these one is Cratægus Crus-galli ; the other C. tanacetifolia. Behind, and partly through these, climbs a very old Noisette Rose— all that now remains of an arched trellis — producing a vast number of bunches of white flowers, six or eight together, and about 1½ in. or 2 in. across. The old gnarled stem of the Rose is scarcely noticeable amongst those of the Thorns till it reaches the top of them, whence it descends between the trees in a regular torrent of blossom, in addition to occupying the topmost boughs of the Cockspur Thorn. A smaller plant of the same Rose has recently been trained up a large Arbor-vitæ and has its stem clothed with Ivy. It is now festooned with snowy flowers hanging down from and against the dark green of the Arbor-vitæ and Ivy.'

' We have,' says a correspondent, ' a collection of Roses, but one of the most attractive is an old double white Ayrshire Rose, growing in a group of common Laurel. We cannot tell how old the plant may be, but it has probably been in its present situation for thirty years, struggling to keep its place among the tall Laurels, sometimes sending out a shoot of white flowers on this side and sometimes on that side of the clump, and then scrambling up to the tops of the tallest limbs and draping them with its blossoms throughout June and July. Nearly three years ago the Laurels were cut down to within 6 feet of the ground, leaving the straggling limbs of the Rose amongst them, and since then it has thriven amazingly, and now seems to gain the mastery, the plant being now over 70 feet round.   Within this space the plant forms an irregular undulating mound, in all parts so densely covered with Roses that not so much as a hand's breadth is left vacant anywhere, and the Laurel branches are quite hidden, and in fact are now dying, smothered by the Rose.   The plant has been a perfect sheet of bloom for a month or more, and there are thousands of buds yet to expand, and hundreds of bunches of buds had been cut just at the opening stage—when they are neater and whiter than a Gardenia—to send away.   Except against walls, there is no need to prune climbing Roses.   Left to themselves, they give the best bloom in deep, strong soil, and with a fair amount of light on all sides.'

CLIMBING ROSE on grass.

AUTUMN CROCUSES in the Wild Garden.

CHAPTER XIII.

SOME RESULTS.

DETAILS of a few of the results obtained, where the
system has been tried, in addition to those already given
of Longleat, may be not without interest. How much
a wild garden intelligently made may effect for a country
seat is shown at Crowsley in Oxfordshire. It is one of
the first-formed wild gardens existing, and in May was
full of charms. No garden yields its beauty so early in
the year, or over a more prolonged season, than the wild
garden, as is abundantly evidenced here. The maker
of this wild garden had no inviting site with which to
deal ; no great variety of surface, no variety of soil for
plants of widely different habitats to be grown ; he had
only a neglected plantation, with a poor gravelly soil

and little variety of surface beyond a few gravel banks thrown up long before. The garden is on each side of a Grass drive, with scattered trees on the one hand and rather shady ground on the other. The most beautiful aspect at the end of May after an ungenial spring, which had not allowed the Pæonies to unfold, was that of the German Irises, with their great Orchid-like blossoms seen everywhere through the wood, clear above the Grass and other herbage—stately flowers that, like the Daffodils, fear no weather, yet with hues that cannot be surpassed by tropical flowers. If this wild garden should teach only effective ways of using the many beautiful Irises in our garden flora, it would do good service. The Irises are perfectly at home in the plantation and among the Grass and wild flowers. When they go out of flower, they will not be in the way as in a ' mixed ' border, but rest in the grass till awakened in spring.

In the wild garden the fairest of our own wild flowers may be happily grouped with like plants from other countries. Here the sturdy Bell-flowered Scilla (S. campanulata) grows wild with our Wood Hyacinth ; the white and pink forms also of the last - named look beautiful here associated with the common well-known form. The earlier kinds of Scilla are past ; they are nice for the wild garden, especially S. bifolia, which thrives freely in woods. The Lily of the Valley did not inhabit the wood before ; it was pleasant to thin out some of its matted tufts in the garden and carry them to the wild garden, where they are now in bloom. The

Solomon's Seal, which is often charming on the fringes of shrubberies, is here arching high over the Woodruff and other woodland flowers, among which it seems a giant, showing fine form with every leaf, and stem, and blossom. The vigour and grace shown by this plant in rich soil are delightful. The greater Celandine (Chelidonium majus) and its double form are very pretty here with their tufts of golden flowers, taking care of them-

CRANE'S BILL, wild, in grass.

selves. The same may be said of the Honesty, the common Columbine, and Allium Moly, an old plant, which is one of the many at home in the wild garden, and better left out of the garden proper. The myriads of Crocus leaves dying off without the indignity of being cut off or tied into bundles as is common in gardens, the dense growth of Aconite and Snowdrop leaves, of coloured and common Primroses and Cowslips, suggest the beauty of this wild garden earlier in spring. The yet unfolded buds on the many groups of Pæonies, promise noble effects early in June; so do the colonies of the splendid Eastern Poppy (Papaver orientale) and the Lilies, and Sweet Williams, and Lupins, which will show their blossoms above or among the summer Grass in due time. The most brilliant effect I have ever seen in any garden was in a corner of this wild garden in summer, when many great oriental Poppies stood in ranks with the Lupins and Columbines, all growing close together in long grass in a green bay of the plantation.

Among the best of the Borageworts here, are the Caucasian Comfrey (Symphytum caucasicum), an admirable wood or copse plant, and red-purple or Bohemian Comfrey (S. bohemicum), which is very handsome. And what lovely effects from the Forget-me-nots—the wood Forget-me-not, and the Early Forget-me-not (M. dissitiflora)—are seen here! where their soft clouds of blue in the Grass are much prettier than when set in the brown earth in a prim border. Here the pushing of the delicate Grass blades through the blue mass, and the way in which the fringes of the tufts mingle with the other plants, are very beautiful.

Some gravel banks are covered with Stonecrops, Saxifrages, and the like, which would, as a rule, have a poor chance in Grass. Some of the prettiest effects of this wild garden result from the way in which dead trees have been adorned. Some of the smaller branches are lopped off, and one or more climbers planted at the base of the tree. Here a Clematis, a climbing Rose, a fine Ivy, a wild Vine, or a Virginian Creeper, has all it requires, a firm support on which it may arrange itself after its own natural habit, without being mutilated; it gives no trouble to the planter, and has fresh ground free to itself. Even when an old tree falls and tosses up a mass of soil and roots the planter is ready with some handsome Bramble or wild Vine to scramble over the stem. Ferns are at home here in the shady corners; all the strong hardy kinds may be so grown, and they look better among the flowers than in the 'hardy Fernery' so called. Even more graceful than the Ferns, and in some cases more useful, because they send up their plume-like leaves very early in the year, are the giant Fennels (Ferula), which grow well here, and hold their own easily among the strongest plants. The common Fennel is also here, but it seeds so freely that it becomes a weed. and overruns plants of greater value. Such plants as Heracleum, Willow Herb, and many others, which not only win, but destroy all their fellows, in the struggle for life, should be planted only in outlying positions, islands, hedges, and small bits of isolated wood or copse, where their effects might be seen in due season, and where they might ramble without destroying. Rabbits—dreaded vermin in the wild garden—are kept out here effectually by means of wire fencing. The presence of these pests prevents all success in the wild garden. To succeed with the wild garden, one should have a good collection of hardy flowers from which it can be supplied. Here one has been formed, consisting of about 1,100 species, mostly arranged in borders. From these, from time to time, over-vigorous and over-abundant kinds may be taken to the wild garden. In a large collection one often finds kinds fit for freedom. The many plants good in all positions may increase in these borders till plentiful enough for planting out in some quantity in the wild garden. The wild garden here has been wholly formed by the owner, who planted with his own hands the plants that now adorn it throughout the year.

Tew Park will long be interesting, from the fact that it was there J. C. Loudon practised agriculture before he began writing the works that were such a marked addition to the garden literature of England. The Grove there is a plantation of fine trees, bordering a wide sweep of grass that varies in width. This grove, unlike much of the rest of the ground, does not vary in surface, or varies but little, so that one of the greatest aids is absent. Originally this now pleasant grove was a dense wood, with Gout-weed mainly on the ground, and troublesome flies in the air. A few years ago the formation of a wild garden was determined upon, and the first operation was the thinning of the wood; light and moving air were let into it, and overcrowded trees removed. It was found, after deeply digging the ground, and sowing the Wood Forget-me-not, that Gout-weed rapidly disappeared. The effect of broad sheets of this Wood Forget-me-not (Myosotis sylvatica) beyond, and seen above, the long waving Grass, gradually receding under the trees, was very beautiful; now (June) its beauty is not so marked as earlier, when, the plants being more compact, the colour was fuller; but one charm of the wild garden is that the very changes

TIGER LILIES in Wild Garden at Great Tew.

of plants from what may be thought their most perfect state of blossom, may be itself a new pleasure instead of a warning that we must cut them down or replace them.

Not to mow is almost a necessity in the wild garden, and as there is often in large gardens much more mown surface than is necessary, many will not regret it. Here the Grass is left unmown in many places. Of course it may be cut when ripe, and most of the spring flowers have past and their leaves are out of danger. Even in parts where no flowers are planted the Grass is left till long enough to cut as meadow. Except where wanted as a carpet, Grass may often be allowed to grow even in the pleasure ground ; quite as good an effect is afforded by unmown as by mown Grass—indeed, better when the long Grass is full of flowers. Three-fourths of the most lovely flowers of cold and temperate regions are companions of the Grass—like Grasses in hardiness, like Grasses in summer life and winter rest, like Grasses in stature. Whatever plants may seem best to associate together in gardens, an immense number—more than two thousand species of those now cultivated—would thrive to perfection among our meadow Grasses, as they do on the Grassy breast of the mountain in many northern lands. Some, like the tall Irises or Columbines, will show their heads clear above the delicate bloom of the Grass ; others, like the Cerastiums, will open their cups below it. The varieties of Columbine in the Grass were perhaps the prettiest flowers at the time of my visit. The white, purplish, and delicately-coloured forms of this charming old plant, just seen above the tops of the long Grass, growing singly, in little groups, or in colonies, formed a June garden of themselves. Established among the Grass, they will henceforward, like it, take care of themselves. The rosy, heart-shaped blooms of the Dielytra spectabilis are seen at some distance through the Grass, and, so grown, furnish a bright and pretty

LARGE-FLOWERED CLEMATIS.

effect. Tree Pæonies succeed, and their great heads of flower quite light up this charming wilderness. Plants of the Goat's Beard Spiræa (S. Aruncus) are very stately and graceful, even now, before they flower, being quite 6 feet high. In the wild garden, apart from the naturalization of free-growing exotics, the establishment of rare British flowers is one of the most interesting occupations; and here, under a Pine tree, the modest, trailing Linnæa borealis of the northern Fir-woods is beginning to spread. The Fox-glove was not originally found in the neighbourhood ; now the ordinary kind and the various other forms of this fine wild flower adorn the woods. In this way also the Lily of the Valley has been planted and is spreading rapidly. Many climbing Roses and various other climbers have been planted at the bases of trees and stumps. A White Indian Clematis here, first trained on a wall, sent up some of its shoots through a tree close at hand, and now the long shoots hang from the tree full of flowers. The large plumes of the nobler hardy Ferns are seen here and there through the trees and Grass, and they are better here among the Grass and flowers, half shaded by trees, than in the 'hardy Fernery.' The wild garden of the future will be also the true home of all the larger hardy Ferns. The rivals of the Ferns in beauty of foliage, the Ferulas, and other hardy plants with beautifully cut foliage, have also their homes in the wild garden. The Welsh Poppy thrives, as might be expected, admirably here, its rich yellow cups just showing above the meadow.

In another part of the grounds there is a high walk quite away from trees, open and dry, with banks on each side—a sun-walk, with Scotch Roses, Brooms, Sun Roses, Rock Roses, and things that love the sun, like the plants of the hot and rocky hillsides of the Mediter-ranean shores. Spanish Broom, Lavenders, Rosemary, Thyme, and Balm, are among the plants that thrive as well on a sunny sandy bank in England as in Italy or Greece.

True taste in the garden is, unhappily, much rarer than many people suppose. No amount of expense, rich collections, good cultivation, large gardens, and plenty of glass, will suffice. A garden of a few acres showing a real love of the beautiful in Nature, as it can be illustrated in gardens, is rare; and when it is seen it is often rather the result of accident than of design. This is partly owing to the fact that the kind of knowledge one wants in order to form a really beautiful garden is very uncommon. No man can do so with few materials. It is necessary to have some knowledge of the wealth of beauty which the world contains for our gardens; and yet this knowledge must not have a leaning, or at any rate but a very partial leaning, towards the Dryasdust. The disposition to 'dry' everything, to concern oneself entirely with nomenclature and classification, is not the gardening spirit —it is the *life* we want. The garden of the late Mr. Hewittson, at Weybridge, had some of the most delightful garden scenes. Below the house, on the slope over the water of Oatlands Park, and below the usual lawn beds and trees, there is a piece of heathy ground—charming beyond any power of the pencil to show. The ground was partially clad with common Heaths with little green paths through them, and naturalized in the warm sandy soil were the Sun Roses which are shown in the foreground of the engraving. Here and there among the Heaths, creeping about in a perfectly natural-looking fashion, too, was the Gentian-

SUN ROSES (Cistus) and other exotic hardy plants among heather, on sandy slope.   (Surrey.)

blue Lithospermum prostratum. Among these groups were the large Evening Primroses and Peruvian Lily (Alstrœmeria), the whole relieved by bold masses of flowering shrubs, so grouped as not to show a trace of formality. All this was done without in the least detracting from the most perfect keeping. The garden is more free from offensive geometrical-twirling, barren expanse of gravelled surface, and all kinds of puerilities —old-fashioned and new-fangled—than any garden I have seen for years.

The following, from a correspondent, shows what may be done with few advantages as to space or situation :—

'We have a dell with a small stream of spring water running through it. When I first came to Brockhurst I found this stream carried underground by a tile culvert, and the valley sides covered with Rhododendrons, the soil between carefully raked and kept free from weeds, so that it was only during springtime that flowers relieved the sombre effect of this primness. After five years this has all been changed into what I think you would call a wild garden, and we have cheerfulness and beauty all the year round.

'In the first place the brooklet was brought to the surface, and its course fringed with marsh plants, such as Marsh Marigolds, Forget-me-nots, Celandines, Irises, Primroses, and Ranunculuses, together with Osmundas, Hart's-tongues, and other Ferns. Many large-growing Carex and large Rushes are also here. Little flats were formed and filled with peat, in which Cypripediums, Trilliums, Orchises, Solomon's Seal, and many rare bog-plants find a home. In the valley we have planted bulbs by thousands—Crocuses, Snowdrops, Daffodils, and Narcissi. The Rhododendrons were thinned and interspersed with Azaleas, and other handsome-foliaged shrubs, to give brightness to the spring flowering, and rich colour to the foliage in autumn. In the spaces between we introduced Wild Hyacinths everywhere, and in patches among these the Red Campion, together with every other pretty wild flower we could obtain—Forget-me-nots, Globe-flowers, Columbines, Anemones, Primroses, Cowslips, Polyanthuses, Campanulas, Golden Rods, &c. We have also planted bulbs very extensively, and as they have been allowed to grow on

WOODRUFF AND IVY

undisturbed we have now large patches of Daffodils, Narcissi, and other spring flowers in great beauty. When we trim the garden all the spare plants are brought here, where they form a reserve, and it is thus gradually getting stocked, and all the bare ground covered with foliage and flowers. Lastly, for autumn blooming we raised large quantities of Foxgloves in every colour, and the larger Campanulas, and these were pricked out everywhere, so that we have, to close the year, a glorious show of Foxglove flowers worth all the trouble. A wild garden of this sort is a very useful reserve ground, where many a plant survives after it has been lost in the borders. The Lily of the Valley and Sweet Violet also flourish here, creeping over heaps of stones, and flower more freely than they do in more open situations. Visitors often say that the dell beats all the rest of the garden for beauty, and it certainly gives less trouble in the attainment.

Wm. Brockbank.'

Brockhurst, Didsbury. (In *Garden.*)

SNOWDROPS, by streamlet.

CHAPTER XIV.

HARDY EXOTIC FLOWERING PLANTS FOR THE WILD GARDEN.

WHEREVER there is room, plants for the Wild Garden should be at first grown in nursery beds to ensure a good supply. The many nursery collections of hardy plants being now more numerous than they were a few years ago, getting the plants is not so difficult as it once was. The sources of supply are these nurseries ; seed houses, which publish lists of hardy plant seeds—many kinds may be easily raised from seed ; botanic gardens, in which many plants are grown that hitherto have not found a place in our flower-gardens ; orchards and cottage gardens in pleasant country places may supply plants from time to time ; and those who travel may bring home seeds or roots of plants they meet with in cool or mountain regions. Bulb and seed-merchants should offer hardy bulbs in large quantities for wild gardening, and at nearly wholesale rates. Few plants, vigorous and hardy in the British Islands without any attention after planting, are included here :—

Bear's Breech, *Acanthus.*—Vigorous perennials with handsome foliage, mostly from Southern Europe. Long cast out of gardens, they are now receiving more attention, and in no position will they look better than planted here and there on the margin of a shrubbery, where the leaves of the Acanthus contrast well with those of the ordinary shrubs or herbaceous vegeta-

tion. Hardy in all soils, they flower most freely in free loamy ground. Not varying very much in character, all obtainable hardy species would group well together. The most vigorous kind at present in cultivation is the one called A. latifolius, which is almost evergreen, and a fine plant when well established. Few plants are more fitted for

THE MONKSHOOD, naturalized.

adorning rough and stony places, as they grow and increase without care, and are, for foliage or bloom, unsurpassed by any of the numerous plants that have been so long neglected because they have not been available in 'flower gardening.'

Monkshood, *Aconitum.*—Tall, handsome perennials, with very poisonous roots, which make it dangerous to plant them in or near gardens. Being vigorous they spread freely, and hold their own amongst herbaceous plants and weeds. Masses of them seen in flower in half-shady places in rich soil give a fine effect. There are many species, nearly all of equal value for the wild garden. Coming from the plains and mountains of Siberia and Northern Europe and America, they are among the hardiest of plants. Spreading groups of Aconites in bloom in open spaces in shrubberies have a finer effect than when the plants are tied into bundles in trim borders. The old blue-and-white kind is charming, and attains stately dimensions in good soil. The species grow in any soil, but on cold heavy ones are often somewhat stunted in growth.

Bugle, *Ajuga.*—Not a very numerous family as represented in gardens, but some of the species are valuable for the wild garden, notably Ajuga genevensis, which thrives freely in ordinary soils in open and half-shady places among dwarf vegetation, and affords beautiful tufts and carpets of blue. It spreads rapidly and is hardy everywhere. The plants mostly come from the cool uplands and hills of the temperate regions of Europe and Asia.

Yarrow, *Achillea.*—A numerous family of hardy plants spread through Northern Asia, Italy, Greece and Turkey, Hungary, but more in Southern than in Central or Northern Europe. In the Alps and Pyrenees numerous species are found. The Golden Yarrows (A. Eupatorium and A. Filipendula) are stately herbaceous plants, with handsome corymbs of yellow flowers attaining a height of 3 feet or 4 feet; growing freely in any soil, they are well worthy of naturalization. Various other kinds would grow quite as well in plantations and rough places as the common Yarrow. The vigorous white-flowered kinds are fine for shrubberies, where their many white heads of flowers give a pleasing effect under the trees in summer. With few exceptions these plants have never been grown out of botanic gardens, many of them being thought too coarse for the mixed border. They are, nevertheless, remarkably beautiful both in flower and foliage, and many effects never before seen in gardens may be obtained by massing them under trees in open shrubberies or copses, as a rule allowing one species to establish itself in each place and assume an easy and broken boundary.

Allium.—Plants scattered in abundance throughout the

THE WHITE NARCISSUS-LIKE ALLIUM, in the orchards of Provence; type of family receiving little place in gardens which may be beautiful for a season in wild places.

northern temperate and alpine regions of Europe and Asia, and also America. Some are so beautiful as to claim a place in gardens notwithstanding their disagreeable odour. It is only in the wild garden, however, that this family finds a fitting home. One of the prettiest effects to produce in the wild garden would be that of the beautiful white Narcissus-like Allium of the south of Europe (A. neapolitanum). The sheets of this in the Lemon orchards of Provence will be remembered by many travellers. It would thrive in warm and sandy soils, and there is an allied species (A. ciliatum) which does well in any soil, gives a similar effect, and produces myriads of star-like white flowers. Singular effects may be produced from species less showy and more curious and vigorous, as, for example, the old yellow A. Moly.

Alstrœmeria.—All who care for hardy flowers must admire Alstrœmeria aurantiaca, especially spreading into healthy masses, and when there is a great variety in the height of the flowering stems. A valuable quality of the plant is, that it spreads freely in any light soil, and is quite hardy. For dry places between shrubs, for dry or sandy banks (either planted or bare), or heathy places, this plant is admirable. I have noticed it thriving in the shade of fir trees. It is interesting as being a South American plant, thriving in warm soils, but often slow and dwarf on cold soils.

Marsh Mallow, *Althœa.*—These are plants rarely seen out of botanic gardens, and yet, from their vigour and showy flowers, may be effective in the wild garden. The common Hollyhock is an Althæa, and in its single form is typical of the vigorous habit and good showy flowers of other rampant species, such as A. ficifolia. A group of these plants would be effective near a wood walk, no flower garden being large enough for their extraordinary vigour.

Alyssum.—In spring every single little shoot of the wide tufts and flakes of these plants sends up a little fountain of small golden flowers. For bare, stony, or rocky banks, and for poor sandy ground, and ruins, they are admirable. Alyssum Wiersbecki and A. saxatile are strong enough to take care of themselves on the margins of shrubberies, &c., where the vegetation is not very coarse, but are best for rocky or stony places, or old ruins, and thrive freely on cottage garden walls in some districts. There are many species, natives of Germany, Russia, France, Italy, Hungary, and Dalmatia; Asia, principally Siberia, the Altai Mountains, Georgia, Persia, and the entire basin of the Caspian, is rich in them.

Windflower, *Anemone.*—A numerous race of dwarf herbs that contribute much to the most beautiful effects of the mountain, wood, and pasture vegetation of all northern and temperate climes. The flowers vary from intense scarlet to the softest blue; many of the exotic kinds would thrive as well in our woodlands and meadows as they do in their own. There is hardly a position they may not adorn—warm, sunny, bare banks, on which the Grecian A. blanda might open its large blue flowers in winter; the tangled copse, where the Japan Windflower and its varieties might make a bold show in autumn; and the grove, where the Apennine Windflower would contrast charmingly with the Wood Anemone so abundantly scattered in our own woods. The Hepaticas should be considered as belonging to the same genus, not forgetting the Hungarian one, A. angulosa. The Hepaticas thrive best and are seen best in half-woody places, where the spring sun may cheer them by passing through the branches, which afterwards become leafy and shade them from the scorching heats of summer.

St. Bruno's Lily, *Anthericum.*— One of the most lovely effects in the alpine meadows of Europe is that of the delicate white flowers of the St. Bruno's Lily in the Grass in early summer, looking like miniature white Lilies. All who have seen it would no doubt like to enjoy the same on their Grassy meadows. The large-flowered or major variety might be tried with advantage in this way, and the smaller-flowered kinds, A. Liliago and its varieties, are pretty. They are not so likely to find favour in gardens as the larger kind, and therefore the wild garden is the home for them, and in it many will admire their graceful habit and numerous flowers. The kinds best worth growing are natives of the alpine meadows of Europe.

Alkanet, *Anchusa.*—Tall herbaceous plants, with numerous flowers of a fine blue, admirable for dotting about in open places in sunny glades in woods or copses. They mostly come from Southern Europe and Western Asia. A. italica and A. capensis are among the most useful. The English Anchusa sempervirens, rare in some districts, is an excellent wild garden plant.

Snapdragon, *Antirrhinum.* — The common Snapdragon and its beautifully spotted varieties are easily naturalized on old walls and ruins by sowing the seed in mossy chinks. Antirrhinum Asarinum, rupestre, and molle do well treated in the same way. Probably many other species would be found good in like places. About two dozen species are known, but comparatively few of these are in cultivation. They mostly come from the shores of the Mediterranean.

Columbine, *Aquilegia.* — Favourite herbaceous plants, generally of various shades of blue and purple, white, and sometimes bright orange. The varieties of the common kind (A. vulgaris), which are very numerous, are those most likely to be naturalized. In bare places in elevated and moist districts some of the beautiful Rocky Mountain kinds would be worth a trial. In places where wild gardens have been formed the effect of Columbines in the Grass has been beautiful—the flowers group themselves in all sorts of pretty ways, showing just above the long Grass. The tall and handsome A. chrysantha of Western America is the most hardy and enduring of the American kinds. The Columbines are a northern and alpine family, most abundant in Siberia.

Wall Cress, *Arabis.*—Dwarf mountain plants, often producing myriads of white flowers, suitable for sandy or rocky ground, where the vegetation is very dwarf. With them may be associated Cardamine trifolia and Thlaspi latifolium, which resemble Arabis in habit and flowers. All these are suited for association with the purple Aubrietia or yellow Alyssum, and in bare and rocky or gravelly places, and old walls.

Sandwort, *Arenaria.*—Of these little plants there are certain kinds that are vigorous and useful, such as A. montana and A.

SIBERIAN COLUMBINE in rocky place.

graminifolia. The small alpine species are charming for rocky places, and as for the little creeping A. balearica, moist rocks or stones suffice for its support. It covers such surfaces with a close carpet of green, dotted with numerous star-like flowers. Some of the smaller species, such as Arenaria cæspitosa, better known as Spergula pilifera, might be grown in gravel and sandy places. In certain positions in large gardens it would be an improvement to allow the very walks or drives to become covered with very dwarf plants—plants which could be walked upon with little injury. The surface would be dry enough, being drained below, and would be more agreeable to the feet.

Asphodel, *Asphodelus.*—The Asphodels are among the plants that have never been popular, the habit of the species being somewhat coarse and the flowering period not long; and yet they are of a distinct order of beauty, which well deserves to be seen in open spaces in shrubberies. The plants are mostly natives of the countries round the Mediterranean, and thrive freely in ordinary soils.

TALL ASPHODEL in copse.

Lords and Ladies, *Arum.*—Mostly a tropical and sub-tropical family, some plants of which grow as far north as Southern Europe. These are quite hardy in our gardens. The Italian Arum deserves a place in the wild garden, from its fine leaves in winter. It should be placed in sheltered places where it would not suffer much from storms. The old Dragon plant (A. Dracontium) grows freely enough about the foot of rocks or walls in sandy or dry peaty places. The nearly-allied Arum Lily (Calla æthiopica) is quite hardy as a water and water-side plant in the southern counties of England and Ireland.

Silkweed, *Asclepias.*— Usually vigorous perennials, with very curious flowers, common in fields and on river banks in North America and Canada, where they sometimes become troublesome weeds. Of the species in cultivation, A. Cornuti and A. Douglasi could be naturalized easily in rich deep soil. The showy and dwarfer Asclepias tuberosa requires very warm sandy soils to flower as well as in its own dry hills. A good many of the hardy species are not introduced ; some of them are water-side plants, such as A. incarnata, the Swamp Silkweed of the United States.

Starwort, *Aster.*— A very large family of vigorous, often beautiful perennials, mostly with bluish or white flowers, chiefly natives of North America. Many of these, of an inferior order of beauty, used to be planted in our mixed borders, which they very much helped to bring into discredit, and they form a very good example of a class of plants for which the true place is the copse, or rough and half-cared-for places in shrubberies and copses, and by wood-walks, where they will grow as freely as any native weeds, and in many cases prove charming in autumn. With the Asters may be grouped the Galatellas, the Vernonias, and also the handsome Erigeron speciosus, which, however, not being so tall, could not fight its way among such coarse vegetation as that in which the Asters may be grown. Associated with the Golden Rods (Solidago)—also common plants of the American woods—the best of the Asters or Michaelmas

Daisies will form a very interesting aspect of vegetation. It is that which one sees in American woods in late summer and autumn when the Golden Rods and Asters are seen in bloom together. It is one of numerous aspects of the vegetation of other countries which the 'wild garden' will make possible in gardens. To produce such effects the plants must, of course, be planted in some quantity, and not repeated all over the place or mixed up with many other things. Nearly 200 species are known, about 150 of which form part of the rich vegetation of North America. These fine plants inhabit that great continent, from Mexico—where a few are found—to the United States and Canada, where they abound, and even up to the regions far north of that quarter of the world.

In my own garden, at Gravetye, many thousands of these Asters were massed in picturesque ways for the first time : almost every kind in cultivation in gardens in broken but effective groups between the cedars, yews, and other evergreen trees near the house. The trees were planted in a much more open way than is customary, thus avoiding a crowded growth. The Asters kept the ground quite furnished and clean, and were often very beautiful in the autumn winds. They were never staked and perfectly hardy they required no attention after planting. As these plantations, however, were really part of the garden, some more attention was given the Starworts than would have been the case in a wild garden ; that is to say that after two or three years in the same place they were moved, to encourage growth and a longer bloom. The more vigorous of the species—and indeed all of them—may be naturalized in open woods or copses, or by river banks and in hedgerows.

Milk Vetch, *Astragalus.*—A numerous family of hardy

plants, little seen in our gardens, though hundreds of them
are hardy, and many of them among the prettiest of the Pea
flowers that adorn the mountains. They are best for rocky
or gravelly soils, or bare banks, though some of the taller
species, like A. galegiformis, are stout enough to take care
of themselves among the larger perennials. This plant is
valuable for its handsome port and foliage, though its flowers
are not such as recommend it for the flower-garden. The
species from the Mediterranean region might be successfully
introduced on banks in our chalk districts and in rocky
places. A. ponticus, a tall kind, and A. monspessulanus,
a dwarf one, are both worth growing.

Masterwort, *Astrantia.*—This is an elegant genus, of
which few species are known, five being European—found in
Italy, Carinthia, Greece, and the centre of Europe—others
from Northern Asia. They are among the few umbellates
with attractive and distinct flowers, and yet they are rarely
seen in gardens. In the wild garden they are quite at home
among the Grass and medium-sized herbaceous plants, and
partial shade prolongs their quaint beauty.

Blue Rock Cress, *Aubrietia.*—Dwarf rock plants, with
purplish flowers, quite distinct in aspect and hue from
anything else grown in our gardens, and rarely perishing
from any cause, except from being overrun by coarser
plants. They are admirable for association with the
Alyssums and Arabises in any position where the vegetation
is very dwarf, or in rocky bare places. There are several
species and varieties, all almost equally suitable, but not
differing much in aspect or stature from each other. The
Aubrietias come chiefly from the mountains of Greece, Asia
Minor, and neighbouring countries. Wherever there is an
old wall, or a sunk fence, or a bare bank, evergreen curtains

may be formed of these plants, and in spring they will be sheeted with purple flowers, no matter what the weather.

Great Birthwort, *Aristolochia Sipho.*—A great climbing plant for covering arbours, banks, stumps of old trees, and also wigwam-like bowers, formed with branches of trees. It is American, and will grow as high as 30 feet ; A. tomentosa is distinct and not so large in leaf. These will scarcely be grown for their flowers ; but for covering stumps or trees they are valuable, and afford a distinct effect.

Virginian Creepers, *Ampelopsis.*—Although this chapter is mostly devoted to herbaceous plants, the Virginian Creeper and its allies are so useful for forming curtains in rocky places, ravines, or over old trees, that they deserve mention here. These plants are not very distant relations of the vine—the wild American vines that are worthy of a place in our groves, garlanding trees as they do in a grand way.

Bamboo, *Bambusa.*—In many parts of England, Ireland, and Wales, various kinds of Bamboos are more hardy, and perhaps near the sea thrive freely. Their beauty is the more precious from their being wholly distinct in habit from any other plants or shrubs that we grow. They are so tall and so enduring that they will thrive among the strongest plants or bushes, and the partial shelter of the thin wood saves their leaves from the effects of violent winds. By quiet Grass walks, in sheltered dells, in the shrubbery, or in little glades in woods, the Bamboos will be at home. The commonest kind is that generally known as Arundinaria falcata (sometimes called Bambusa gracilis) ; but others, such as Bambusa Metake, B. Simmonsi, and B. viridis-glaucescens, are of equal or greater value. They all delight in rich, light, and moist soils, and in our country some shelter helps them.

Baptisia.—A strong Lupin-like plant seldom grown in gardens, but beautiful when in bloom for its long blue racemes of pea flowers, growing 3 to 4 feet high; it will hold its own in strong soil.

Borage, *Borago.*—A genus seldom seen out of Botanic gardens, where they form part of the usual distressing arrangements honoured with the name of 'scientific.' Among the best kinds for our purpose are B. cretica and B. orientalis; even the well-known annual kind will be found a pretty plant, naturalized in stony places. old quarries, and the like.

Bell-flower, *Campanula.*—Beautiful and generally blue-flowered herbs, varying from a few inches to 5 feet in height, and abundant in northern and temperate countries. All the medium-sized and large kinds thrive very well in rough places, woods, copses, or shrubberies, among grasses and other herbaceous plants; while those smaller in size than our own Harebell (C. rotundifolia) are quite at home, and very pretty, on any arid or bare surfaces, such as sandy banks, chalk pits, and even high up on old walls. In such positions the seeds need only to be scattered. C. rapunculoides and C. lamiifolia do finely in shrubberies or copses, as, indeed, do all the tall-growing kinds, and where there are white varieties they should be secured. Many people will begin to see the great beauty of this family for the first time when they have them growing among the grass— the effect is far more beautiful than that which they show in the garden border.

Red Valerian, *Centranthus ruber.*—This showy plant is seen best only on banks, rubbish-heaps, or old walls, in which positions it endures much longer than on the level ground, and becomes a long-lived perennial with a shrubby base. Grows apace on old bridges, banks, chalk pits, and on stone heaps.

Knap-weed, *Centaurea.*—Vigorous perennial or annual plants, seldom so pretty as autumn-sown plants of our corn bluebottle (C. Cyanus). They are scarcely important enough for borders; hence the wild garden is the place for them. Among the best are macrocephala, montana, babylonica, and uniflora, the last being more suitable for banks.

Mouse-ear, *Cerastium.*—Dwarf plants with many white flowers. Half a dozen or more of the kinds have silvery leaves, and will grow in any position where they are not choked by coarser plants.

The foliage of the MEADOW SAFFRON in Spring.

Wallflower, *Cheiranthus.* — The varieties of the common Wallflower have great beauty for rocky places and old walls. The clear yellow Erysimum ochroleucum is very like a wallflower in type, and thrives well in dry sandy places. With these might be associated Vesicaria utriculata.

Meadow Saffron, *Colchicum.*—In addition to the Meadow Saffron, dotted over the moist fields in various parts of England, there are several other species that could be naturalized in grassy places, and they would be useful where plants that flower in autumn are sought.

Crocus.—One or two kinds of Crocus are naturalized in England. They should not be placed where coarse vegetation would choke them up or prevent the sun getting to their flowers and leaves. Some of the pretty varieties of vernus are well worth planting in grassy places and on sunny slopes. C. Imperati is an early kind, and the autumnal Croci are charming.

'In the plantations here,' writes a friend, 'on each side of a long avenue, we have the common Crocus in every shade of purple (there are scarcely any yellow ones) growing literally in hundreds of thousands. We have no record of when the roots were originally planted (and the oldest people about the estate say they have always been the same); but they grow so thickly that it is impossible to step where they are without treading on two or three flowers. The effect produced by them in spring is magnificent. I have transplanted a good many roots to the wild garden, to the great improvement of the size of the blooms ; they are so matted together in the shrubberies, and have remained so long in the same place, that the flowers are small.'

In my own garden the prettiest early effects are those of Crocuses in the grass, which come up year after year without attention of any kind, and which no manure or 'compost' of any kind has once touched.

Virgin's Bower, *Clematis.*— Mostly climbing or trail-

THE WHITE-FLOWERED EUROPEAN CLEMATIS (C. erecta).

ing plants, free, often luxuriant, sometimes rampant, in habit, with bluish, violet, purple, white, or yellow flowers, and sometimes deliciously fragrant. They are best suited for covering stumps, planting on rocky places, among low shrubs in copses, for draping over the faces of rocks, sunny banks, or the brows of sunk fences, covering objectionable railings, rough bowers, chalk pits, hedges, &c., and occasionally for isolating in large tufts in open spaces where their effect could be seen from a distance. Not particular as to soil, the stronger kinds will grow in any ground, but the large-flowered new hybrids will thrive best in warm, rich, deep soil. C. Viorna, C. flammula, montana, campaniflora, Viticella, and cirrhosa, must not be omitted from a selection of the wild kinds.

Dwarf Cornel, *Cornus canadensis.*—This charming little plant, beautiful from its white bracts, thrives in moist, sandy, or peaty spots, in which our native heaths—Mitchella repens, Linnæa borealis, and the Butterworts would be likely to thrive.

Mocassin Flower, *Cypripedium spectabile.*— The handsomest of hardy orchids, found far north in America, and thriving perfectly in England and Ireland in deep rich vegetable soil. In places where the soil is not naturally peat or rich vegetable matter this fine plant will succeed on the margins of beds of rhododendrons, &c. It should be sheltered by surrounding bushes, and be in a moist position. Others of the genus, and various other hardy orchids, are worthy of naturalization; the mocassin flower is the best as well as the most easily tried.

Sowbread, *Cyclamen.*—It was the sight of a grove nearly covered with Cyclamen hederæfolium, near Montargis, in France, that first led me to think of how many plants might be tried in like ways. Both C. hederæfolium and C. europæum may be naturalized with ease on light, loamy, or other warm soil. C. vernum, C. Coum, and C. repandum, are also well worthy of trial. Nothing can be more agreeable to the lover of hardy plants than endeavouring to naturalize these charming flowers, now rarely seen out of the greenhouse. The best positions would be among dwarf shrubs, that would afford slight shelter, on banks or sunny open spots in copses or woods. Bare or dug borders they abhor, and a sunny warm exposure should be chosen. In the case of C. hederæfolium (and perhaps some of the

CYCLAMENS in the wild garden ; from nature.

others) ground under trees, bare, or with a very scant vegetation, would do quite well if the soil were free and warm.

The Giant Sea-kale, *Crambe.*— C. cordifolia is a fine perennial, but its place is on the turf in rich soil. It has enormous leaves, and small whitish flowers in panicles. It is one of the finest plants in a wild garden in Oxfordshire of about 5 acres, associated with Rheums, Ferulas, Gunneras, Centaurea babylonica, Arundo Donax, and Acanthus.

Bindweed, *Calystegia.*—Climbers, with handsome white or rosy flowers, often too vigorous to be agreeable in gardens. C. dahurica, larger than the common kind, is handsome trailing through shrubs, in rough places, or over old stumps.

The pretty little Rosy Bindweed that one meets often upon the shores of the Mediterranean is here depicted at home in an English garden, creeping up the leaves of an Iris in Mr. Wilson's garden at Heatherbank, Weybridge Heath.

A SOUTH EUROPEAN BINDWEED creeping up the stems of an Iris in an English garden.

We possess a great privilege in being able to grow the fair flowers of so many regions in our own. This beautiful pink Bindweed is, so to speak, the representative in the south of our own Rosy Field Bindweed, but it is perfectly hardy and free in our own soils. Its botanical name is Convolvulus althæoides. I put the Great Bindweed in the banks when forming fences, as in these it is a harmless as well as a beautiful 'weed.'

Marsh Calla, *Calla palustris.*— A creeping Arum-like plant, with white flowers showing above a low carpet of glossy leaves, admirable for naturalization in muddy places, moist bogs, on the margins of ponds.

Rosy Coronilla, *Coronilla varia.*—On grassy banks, stony heaps, rough rocky ground, spreading over slopes or any like positions. A very fine plant for naturalization, thriving in any soil.

Giant Scabious, *Cephalaria.*—Allied to Scabious but seldom grown. They are worth a place for their fine vigour alone, and the numerous pale yellow flowers will be admired by those who do not limit their admiration to showy colours.

Coral-wort, *Dentaria.*—Showy perennials, the purplish or white flowers of which look like a stock-flower, are distinct in habit and bloom, and too rarely seen in our gardens; they will be found to thrive well and look well in peat soil beneath rhododendrons, and towards the margins of clumps of American shrubs.

Leopard's Bane, *Doronicum.*—Stout, or dwarf perennials, hardy, free, and with very showy flowers; well suited for naturalization among herbaceous vegetation, in any position where the beauty of their early bloom can be enjoyed.

American Cowslip, *Dodecatheon.*— All who care for hardy flowers admire the beautiful American cowslip (D. Meadia), found in rich woods in Pennsylvania, Ohio, to Wisconsin and south-westward, in America. This would be a charming plant to naturalize on rich and light sandy loams, among dwarf herbs, low shrubs, &c., in sheltered and sunny spots. Jeffrey's American cowslip (D. Jeffreyanum), a vigorous kind, is also worth a trial.

Fumitory, *Fumaria, Dielytra.*— Plants with graceful leaves and gay flowers suited for association with dwarf plants on open banks, except D. spectabilis, which in deep peat or other rich soil will grow a yard high. The little Fumaria bulbosa is one of the dwarf plants that thrive under the branches of trees, and Corydalis lutea thrives in almost every position from the top of an old castle to the bottom of a well shaft. I saw Dielytra eximia naturalized in Buckhurst Park, in a shrubbery, the position being shady. Its effect was charming, the plumy tufts being dotted over with flowers, it thrives and spreads freely in shady spots. The blossoms, instead of being of the usual crimson hue, were a delicate pale rose, no doubt owing to the shade ; and, as they drooped over the graceful leaves, they looked like snowdrops of a faint rosy hue.

Delphinium, *Perennial species.*—Tall and beautiful plants, with flowers of many exquisite shades of blue and purple. They are well suited for rich soil in glades, thin shrubberies, or among masses of dwarf shrubs, above which their fine spikes of bloom might here and there arise.

One of the prettiest effects I have ever seen among naturalized plants was a colony of tall Larkspurs (Delphiniums). Portions of old roots of various kinds had been trimmed off where a bed of these plants was being dug, and in the autumn the refuse had been thrown into a near shrubbery, far in among the shrubs and tall trees. Here they grew in half-open spaces, which were so far from the margin that they were not dug and were not seen. When I saw the Larkspurs in flower they were certainly the loveliest things that one could see. They were more beautiful than they are in borders or beds, not growing in such close stiff tufts, and they mingled with and were relieved by the trees above and the shrubs around. This suggests that we might make wild gardens from the mere parings and thinnings of the borders in autumn, where there is a collection of hardy plants.

Pink, *Dianthus.*—Beautiful dwarf mountain plants, with flowers mostly of shades of rose, sometimes sporting into other colours in gardens. The finer alpine kinds would be likely to thrive only on bare stony ground, and with plants of like size. The bright D. neglectus would thrive in any ordinary soil. Some of the kinds in the way of our own D. cæsius grow well on old walls and ruins, as does the single carnation ; indeed, many kinds of pink would thrive on old walls far better than on the ground.

Foxglove, *Digitalis.*—It need not be said here that our own stately Foxglove should be seen in the wild garden, in districts where it does not naturally grow wild ; there are a number of exotic species for which a place might be found— some of them are not very satisfactory elsewhere. The most showy hardy flowers of midsummer are the Foxglove and the French Willow (Epilobium angustifolium), and in rough places in plantations their effect is beautiful. In such half-shady places the Foxglove thrives best ; and, as the French Willow is too rampant a plant for the garden proper, the place for it too is the wild garden. It is a most showy plant, and masses of it may be seen great distances off. The spotted varieties of the Foxglove should be sown as well as the ordinary wild form.

A SEA HOLLY ; Eryngium.

Hemp Agrimony, *Eupatorium.* —Vigorous perennials, with white or purple fringed flowers. Some of the American kinds might well be associated with our own wild one—the white kinds, like aromaticum and ageratoides, being beautiful and distinct.

Sea Holly, *Eryngium.*— Distinct and beautiful perennials, with usually spiny leaves, and flowers in heads, sometimes surrounded by a bluish involucrum, the stems of a fine amethystine blue. They are handsome on margins of shrubberies and near wood-walks, thrive in ordinary free soil, and will take care of themselves among grasses and all but the most vigorous plants. They often come freely from self-sown seed and may be easily naturalized on warm soils and in sunny places.

Heath, *Erica,* *Menziesia.*—The brilliant Erica carnea is so charming that it well deserves naturalization among our native kinds. The beautiful St. Daboec's heath (Menziesia polifolia), found wild in the west of Ireland, is to the majority of English gardens an exotic plant. It will grow almost anywhere in peaty soil. In the country place no kind of gardening is more delightful than the growth in rather bold groups and masses of all hardy Heaths, native or other. It is gardening that may be done in a bold and careless way, and the growth after a few years left to mingle with the grass and other vegetation around. The Heaths beds after a year or two's growth look well throughout the year, and are often beautiful with bloom. Such bold groups would seldom come into the flower-garden, and they are best placed by grass-walks in the pleasure ground, preferring open and raised ground. The natural soil for such plants would seem to be peat, but it is not necessary for their culture. At Gravetye where there is no peat I planted many Heaths which did well.

Barren - wort, *Epimedium.*—Interesting perennials, with pretty flowers, and finely formed leaves. They like peaty or free moist soils, among low shrubs or on rocky banks. The variety called E. pinnatum elegans, when in deep peat soil, forms tufts of leaves nearly a yard high, and in spring bears long racemes of handsome yellow flowers.

Globe Thistle, *Echinops.*—Large perennials of fine port, from 3 feet to 6 feet high, with spiny leaves and numerous flowers in spherical heads. These thrive in almost any position, and hold their ground amid the coarsest vegetation. Of a 'type' distinct from that of our native plants, they are also

well fitted for naturalization—E. exaltatus and E. ruthenicus
are among the best kinds.

May-Flower, *Epigœa repens.*—A small creeping shrub,
with pretty and fragrant flowers, which come soon after the
melting of the snow in N. America, and are there as welcome
as the hawthorn with us. In its native country it inhabits
woods, mostly in the shade of pines ; and wherever I saw it,
it seemed to form a carpet under three or four layers of
vegetation,— that is to say, it was beneath pines, medium-
sized trees, tall bushes, and dwarf scrub, the plant itself was
not more than one or two inches high. It can be naturalized
in pine woods on a sandy soil.

Dog's-tooth Violet, *Erythronium.*—This beautiful plant,
some years ago rarely seen in our gardens, adorns many
a dreary slope in the Southern Alps, and there is no difficulty
in the way of adding its charms to the wild garden.

The Winter Aconite, *Eranthis hyemalis.* - Classed among
British plants but really naturalized. Its yellow buttons
peeping through the moss and grass in snowdrop time form
one of the prettiest aspects of our garden vegetation in spring.
It will grow almost anywhere, and is one of the plants that
thrive under the spreading branches of summer-leafing trees,
as it blooms and ripens its leaves before the buds open on
the beech. On many lawns, spring gardens might be formed
by planting some spring-flowering plants that finish their
growth before the trees are in leaf. Another advantage of
such positions is, that the foliage of the trees prevents coarse
plants taking possession of the ground, and therefore these
little spring plants have the ground to themselves, and wander
into natural little groups in the moss and grass. The winter
Aconite does not thrive in some cool soils.

Plantain Lilies, *Funkia.*— The conditions in the wild

garden are sometimes more suitable to many plants than borders, the plants remaining longer in bloom in the shade and shelter of shrubby places than when exposed. As an instance of this, I saw Funkia cœrula showing great size and beauty in a shady drive at Beauport, near Battle. The plant was over a yard high, and bore many stately stems hung with blue flowers. The Plantain Lilies are plants for the wild garden, not being liable to the accidents that are fatal to Lilies and other plants exposed to the attacks of slugs and rabbits.

Groups of SIEBOLD'S PLANTAIN LILY.

Snake's-head, *Fritillaria.*— The beautiful British Snake's-head (F. Meleagris) grows wild, as most people know, in meadows in various parts of England, and should be established in the meadows of many a country seat. Various other Fritillarias not so pretty as this, and of a peculiar livid dark hue, which is not likely to make them popular in gardens, would be worthy of a position also. Of such is F. tristis, and the Crown Imperial would do on the fringes of shrubberies. The Golden Fritillary is charming, and when plentiful will be lovely in the wild garden.

Giant Fennel, *Ferula.*—Noble herbaceous plants of the parsley family, with exquisitely cut leaves ; forming magnificent tufts of verdure, like the most finely-cut ferns. The leaves rise very early in spring, and go at the end of summer, and the best way to plant them is in places occupied by spring flowers, among which they give a fine effect. With the Giant Fennels might be grouped various other plants of this distinct family of plants, so far very little seen in gardens.

Ferns.—No plants may be naturalized with more charming effect than ferns. The Royal ferns, of which the bold foliage is reflected in the marsh waters of Northern America, will do well in the many places where our own royal fern thrives. The graceful Maidenhair fern of the rich woods of the Eastern States and Canada thrives in any cool place, or dyke, or in a shady wood, but the soil must be leafy and good. The small ferns that find a home on arid alpine cliffs may be established on old walls and ruins. Cheilanthes odora, which grows on the sunny sides of walls in Southern France, might be grown in the south of England, the spores to be sown in mossy chinks of the walls. The climbing fern Lygodium palmatum, which I saw with great pleasure running through native shrubs in cold New Jersey, and which goes as far north as cold Massachusetts, will climb up the undershrubs in England. There is no fern of the numbers that inhabit the northern regions of Europe, Asia, and America, that may not be tried with confidence. One could form a rich and stately type of fern vegetation without employing one of our native kinds at all, though the best way will be to associate all so far as their habits will permit. Treat them boldly ; put strong kinds out in glades ; imagine colonies of Daffodils among the Oak and Beech Ferns, fringed by early Aconite, in the spots overshadowed by the branches of summer-leafing trees. There are few kinds of gardening more interesting than naturalizing the fine hardy ferns of North America. Those having peaty and leafy soils have a great advantage, as many of the plants grow in these soils natur-ally; though the ferns will often grow in loamy soils they do not endure so long or spread so rapidly. The great ferns, like the Feather Ferns that live in the ditches and wet hollows in American woods, are not so difficult, and will grow in any moist deep peat.

Geranium, *Geranium, Erodium.*—Handsome perennials, mostly with bluish, pinkish, or deep rose flowers. Some of the stouter kinds of the hardy geraniums, such as G. ibericum and G. Armenum, are the very plants to take care of themselves in

A hardy GERANIUM.

open places. With them might be grown the fine Erodium Manescavi; and where there are very bare places, on which they would not be overrun by coarser plants, the smaller Erodium, such as E. romanum.

Goat's Rue, *Galega.*—Tall and graceful perennials, with numerous pink, blue, or white flowers, G. officinalis and its white variety are among the pretty tall border flowers, and they are useful for planting in rough places, as is also the blue G. orientalis and G. biloba, being all free growers.

Gypsophila, *Gypsophila.*—Neat perennials, hardy, and with myriads of flowers, mostly small, and of a pale pinkish hue. They are best suited for rocky or sandy ground, or even old ruins, or any position where they will not be smothered by coarser vegetation. Like them in character is the pretty little Tunica Saxifraga, which grows on the tops of old walls and sand heaps in Italy and in Southern Europe, and will thrive on bare places with us.

Gentian, *Gentiana.*—Dwarf, and usually evergreen, alpine or high-pasture plants, with large and numerous flowers often handsome, and frequently of the most vivid blue. The large G. acaulis (Gentianella) would grow as freely in moist places on any of our own mountains as it does on its native hills; indeed, it would flourish in all moist loams, where it could not be choked by coarse and taller subjects. The tall Willow Gentian (G. asclepiadea) is a handsome plant, which, in the mountain woods of Switzerland, I have often seen blooming among long grass in shade of trees, and this fact is suggestive as to its use in this country.

Snowdrops, *Galanthus.*—The charms of our own Snowdrop when naturalized in the grass are well known to all, but many of the new kinds, such as G. Elwesi and G. plicatus, have claims also in that respect, all of which would be as easily naturalized as the common Snowdrop. For some account of the various kinds of Snowdrop that have come into our gardens of recent years see the article in the ' English Flower-garden.'

Cow Parsnips, *Heracleum.*— Giant herbaceous plants, mostly from Northern Asia, with huge leaves, and umbels (sometimes a foot across) of white or whitish flowers. They are very suitable for rough places on the banks of rivers or artificial water, islands, or for any place where bold foliage may be desired. In planting them it should be borne in mind that their foliage dies down and disappears at the end of summer. When established they often sow themselves, so that seedling plants in abundance may be picked up around them; but it is important not to allow them to become giant weeds. To prevent this, it may, in certain positions, be desirable to prevent them seeding.

Day Lily, *Hemerocallis.*—Vigorous plants of the Lily order, with long leaves and large and showy red-orange or yellow flowers, often scented delicately. There are two types, one large and strong like H. flava and H. fulva, the other short and somewhat fragile like H. graminea. The larger kinds are valuable plants for the 'Wild Garden,' thriving in any rich soil.

Christmas Rose, *Helleborus.*—Stout dwarf perennials, with showy blooms appearing in winter and spring when flowers are rare, and with handsome leathery leaves. They thrive in almost any soil; but to get their early bloom good, it is well to place them on sunny banks in groups, and not far from the eye. They form beautiful ornaments near wood walks, where the spring sun can reach them. There are various kinds useful for naturalization, especially on warm chalky soils.

Sun Rose, *Helianthemum.*—Dwarf spreading shrubs, bearing myriads of flowers in a variety of colour. The most satisfactory way of employing these in our gardens is to naturalize them on banks or slopes in the half-wild parts of our pleasure grounds, where there is sandy or warm soil. They are best suited for chalk or rocky districts, where they thrive and make a brilliant display.

Perennial Sunflower, *Helianthus, Rudbeckia, Silphium.*—Stout and very tall perennials with showy yellow flowers, the best known of which is Helianthus multiflorus fl. pl., of which plenty may be seen in Euston Square and other places in London. As a rule these are all better fitted for rough places than for gardens, where, like many other plants mentioned in these pages, they will tend to form a vigorous herbaceous covert. H. rigidus is a brilliantly showy plant, running very freely at the root, and an excellent subject for naturalization. H. giganteus, common in thickets and swamps in America, and growing as high as 10 feet, is also desirable. The showy and larger American Rudbeckias, such as laciniata, triloba, and also the small but showy hirta, belong to the same type. All these plants, and many others of the tall yellow composites that one sees among herbaceous vegetation in America, would give showy effects in autumn, and might perhaps interest those who only visit their country seats at that time of year. The Silphiums, especially the compass plant (S. laciniatum), and the cup plant (S. perfoliatum), are in general character like Helianthus.

St. John's Wort, *Hypericum.*—The well-known St. John's Wort does only too freely in many places ; there is scarcely one of its numerous brethren which will not thrive in rough places, in any soil. They have all the same bright yellow flowers as the St. John's Wort, and are nearly all taller. Some of the newer kinds have handsome flowers like the St. John's Wort. It should be noted that the common St. John's Wort so exhausts the soil of moisture that it sometimes is the cause of the death of trees. Many places have too much of it, as they also have of the common Laurel.

Rocket, *Hesperis.*—The common single Rocket (Hesperis matronalis) is a showy plant in copse or shrubbery, and very easily raised from seed.

Evergreen Candytuft, *Iberis.*— Compact little evergreens, forming spreading bushes from 3 inches to 15 inches high, and sheeted with white flowers in spring and early summer. There are no plants better for naturalization in open or stony places, or, indeed, in any position where the vegetation is not strong enough to overrun them. They, however, attain greatest beauty when fully exposed to the sun, and are admirable for every kind of rocky or stony ground and banks.

Iris, *Fleur de Lis.*—These plants, once so well known in our gardens, rivalling (or rather exceeding) the lilies in beauty, are varied and numerous enough to make a wild garden by themselves. The many beautiful varieties of germanica will grow in almost any soil, and may be planted in woods, copses, by wood walks, or near the margin of water, though the water-rat often eats the roots. I. sibirica will grow in the water, as will the Japanese and the beautiful Asiatic Irises such as I. aurea and I. Monnieri. On the other hand, I. pumila, and the varieties of germanica, are often seen on the tops of old walls and thatched roofs, in France, flowering well.

Common Lupine, *Lupinus polyphyllus.*—Amidst the handsomest hardy plants, grouped where they may be seen from grass drives or wood walks, or in any position or soil. Excellent for islets or on river banks, in the soil of which it spreads freely.

Honesty, *Lunaria.*—This, which approaches the Stocks in the aspect of its fine purplish violet flowers, is one of the best plants for naturalization. Sows itself freely in dryish ground or on chalk banks, and is one of the prettiest plants in early summer.

Lily, *Lilium.*—There are hardy lilies that may be naturalized. The places that these grow in, from the high meadows of Northern Italy, dotted with the orange lily, to the woody gorges of the Sierras in California, rich with tall and handsome kinds, are such as make their chances in copses and rough grassy places, hopeful. In woods where

there is rich vegetable soil the fine American lilies will do
The European lilies, dotted in the grass in the rough unmown
glades, would not grow nearly so large as they do in the
rich borders of our cottage gardens; but the effect of the
single large blooms of the orange lily just level with the tops
of the grass, in early summer, where it grows wild, is as good
as any effect it gives in gardens. Along the bed of small
rivulets, in the bottom of narrow gorges densely shaded by
great Pines, Arbutus trees 60 feet high, and handsome
evergreen oaks on the Sierras of California, I saw in
autumn numbers of lily stems 7, 8, and 9 feet high, so
one could imagine what pictures the flowers formed in early
summer. No mode of cultivating lilies in gardens is equal
to that of dotting them through beds of rhododendrons
and other American plants usually planted in peat, the soil
of these beds, usually and very unwisely left to the rhododendrons alone, being peculiarly suited to the majority of the
lily tribe. As for Lilies in the wild garden, Mr. G. F.
Wilson sent me a stem of Lilium superbum, 11½ feet high,
grown in a rich woody bottom; this fine lily—the swamp
lily of North America—should be planted in rich boggy
bottoms where these occur in the wild garden.

Snowflake, *Leucojum*.—I have rarely seen anything more
beautiful than a colony of the summer Snowflake on the
margin of a tuft of rhododendrons at Longleat. Some of the
flowers were on stems nearly 3 feet high, the partial shelter
of the bushes and good soil causing the plants to be
unusually vigorous. Both the spring and summer Snowflakes (L. vernum and L. æstivum) are valuable plants for
wild grassy places, and the last grows freely in the good soil
in the islets in the Thames near Wargrave.

Gentian Lithosperm, *Lithospermum prostratum*.— A very

distinct and pretty plant, with many flowers of as fine a blue as any gentian. Thrives in any deep sandy soil, and in such well deserves naturalization among dwarf rock plants, in sunny spots.

Lychnis.—Handsome perennials, with showy blooms, mostly of a brilliant rose or scarlet colour. If the type were represented by the rose campion only it would

be a valuable one, as this is a beautiful plant in dry soils, on which it does not perish in winter. The Lychnises are most fitted for association with medium-sized perennials, in open places and in rich soil.

Honeysuckle, *Lonicera.*—Such favourites as these must not be omitted. Any kind of climbing Honeysuckle will find a happy home in the wild garden, either rambling over stumps or hedgerows,

EVERLASTING PEA. creeping up stem in shrubbery.

or planted by themselves on banks. Our woods are graced by our wild Honeysuckles, and where garden varieties or new kinds of Honeysuckle from other countries are plentiful, it is well to add them to the wild garden.

Pea, *Lathyrus.*—Most cultivators of flowers are aware of the rambling habits of the greater number of plants of the pea tribe, but in that particular L. pyrenaicus eclipses them all. It produces an immense quantity of bright orange blossoms, but a strong plant of this species will ramble over, and by its density of growth prevent every plant and shrub that comes within its reach from thriving; indeed, it is a greater rambler than the Hop, the Bindweed, or the Bryony, and is very handsome. Tying up or training such a plant is out of the question; but there are many rough places in the wild garden where it would be quite at home. Every kind of Everlasting Pea is excellent for the wild garden, either for scrambling over hedgerows, stumps, or growing among the grass.—J. W. in *Garden.*

Monkey-flower, *Mimulus.*—'Wandering one day in the neighbourhood of "Gruigfoot," a queer-shaped hill in Linlithgowshire, my eye was attracted by a small burn whose banks were literally jewelled throughout its visible course with an unfamiliar yellow flower. A nearer approach showed me that it was the garden Mimulus (Monkey-flower), the seed of which must have escaped from some cottage garden, and established itself here, in the coldest part of the British Isles. I took the hint, and have naturalized it by the banks of a small stream which runs at the foot of my garden, and I strongly recommend your readers to do the same. It mingles charmingly with the blue Forget-me-not.'—S. in *Garden.*

Grape Hyacinth, *Muscari.*—These free and hardy little bulbs are easily naturalized and very handsome, with their little spikes of flowers of many shades of blue. At Gravetye I used to throw the bulbs in little hollows in grassy places, and then fill up level with a couple of inches of soil, thus saving the trouble of lifting the turf to plant. We had some very pretty effects, my only trouble was in not being able to get these things by the million.

Forget-me-not, *Myosotis.*—There is one exotic species, M. dissitiflora, not inferior in beauty to any of our handsomest native kinds, and well worthy of naturalization everywhere. It thrives best on moist and sandy or rocky soil.

Molopospermum cicutarium.—A very fine plant, with large deeply-divided leaves of a lively green colour, forming a dense irregular bush. Many of the umbellate plants, while very elegant, perish by the end of June, but this is firmer in character, of a fine rich green, growing more than 3 feet high. It is hardy, and increased by seed or division, and loves a deep moist soil, but will thrive in any good garden soil. It is a fine plant for grouping with other hardy and graceful-leaved plants.

Type of fine-leaved umbellate plants seldom grown in gardens.

Stock, *Matthiola.*—Showy flowers, mostly fragrant, peculiarly well suited for old ruins, chalk pits, and stony banks. Some of the annual kinds are pretty. With the Stocks may be associated the single rocket (Hesperis matronalis), which thrives on woody banks and in copses.

Bee Balm, *Monarda.*—Large and very showy herbaceous plants, with scarlet or purple flowers, beautiful in American and Canadian woods in autumn, and good plants for naturalization in woods and shrubberies, copses, or anywhere among medium-sized vegetation. They thrive best in light or well-drained soils. Few plants have given me more pleasure than wide groups of the scarlet Bee Balm, which are splendidly effective, and form pictures from various points of view in the same place. Even in the broiling summer of 1893 we enjoyed their beauty for many weeks.

Mallow, *Malva, Althœa, Malope, Kitaibelia, Callirhoë, Sida.*—Plants of several distinct genera may be included under this type, and from each very showy plants.

They are for the most part too coarse for gardens generally; but among the taller vegetation in rough shrubberies, and glades in woods, they give good effect. Some of the Malvas are vigorous-growing plants, mostly with rosy flowers. The Althæas, close allies of the common single hollyhock, are fine, as are also the Sida and Kitaibelia vitifolia. The Malopes are among the best of the annual flowers. The Callirhoës are dwarf, handsome trailers, brilliant too, and are the only ones of the type that should be planted amidst dwarf vegetation, as all the others are of vigorous character.

THE BEE BALM, Monarda. American wood plant.

Mulgedium Plumieri.—A plant of distinct port, with purplish-blue blossoms. Till recently it was generally seen in botanic gardens only, but it has many merits as a wild garden plant, and for groups in quiet green corners of pleasure grounds or shrubberies. It does best in rather rich ground, and in such will pay all who plant it, being a hardy and long-lived perennial. The foliage is sometimes over a yard long, and the flower-stems over 6 feet high in good soil.

Water Lily, *Nymphæa and Nuphar.*—Two noble North American plants well deserve naturalization in our waters, associated with our own beautiful white water lilies—the large Nuphar advena, which thrusts its great leaves well out of the water in many parts of North America, and the sweet-scented Nymphæa odorata, which floats in crowds on many of the pine-bordered lakes and lakelets of New England, looking very like our own water lily. These and the new and beautiful hybrid water lilies have been dealt with fully in the Chapter on Water Plants.

Daffodil, *Narcissus.*—Most people have seen the common daffodil in a wild state in our woods and fields. Apart from varieties, there are more than a score of species of daffodil that could be naturalized quite as easily as this in all parts of these islands. Of all the planting I have ever made, the planting of these in the grass has given the greatest pleasure and the most lasting. They were put in by thousands, in the meadows mown for hay as well as in the less shaven parts of the pleasure ground, and no kind that we tried failed save the Bayonne Daffodil. We did not try the southern and Hoop Petticoat kinds, as the soil was not warm or sandy enough.

Bitter Vetch, *Orobus.*—Banks, grassy unmown margins of wood-walks, rocks, fringes of shrubberies, and like places, with deep and sandy loam, well drained, will grow the beautiful spring Bitter Vetch or any of its varieties or allies perfectly.

Evening Primrose, *Œnothera.*—Among the handsomest of hardy flowers. The yellow species, and varieties allied to the common Evening Primrose (Œ. biennis), may be readily naturalized in any soil. These noble and fragrant flowers are easily grown and beautiful. They, however, from their boldness, are suited for shrubberies, copses, and the like, sowing themselves freely.

Cotton Thistle, *Onopordon.*—Large thistles, with very handsome hoary and silvery leaves, and purplish flowers on fiercely-armed stems. No plants are more distinct than these, and they thrive freely in rough open places and on rubbish heaps, and usually come up freely from self-sown seeds.

Star of Bethlehem, *Ornithogalum.*—Various handsome hardy species of this genus will thrive as well as the common Star of Bethlehem in any turf; other less popular kinds have a quiet graceful beauty, and not being generally admitted to the gay company of showy tulips and the like, there is all the more reason to give them a home in the grass.

Creeping Forget-me-not, *Omphalodes.*—The creeping Forget-me-not (Omphalodes verna) is one of the prettiest plants to be naturalized in woods, copses, or shrubberies, running about with freedom in moist soil. It is more compact in habit and lives longer on good soils than the other Forget-me-nots, and should be naturalized round every country place.

Wood Sorrel, *Oxalis.*—Dwarf plants with clover-like leaflets and pretty rosy or yellow flowers. Two of the species in cultivation, viz. O. Bowieana and O. floribunda, thrive on sandy soils amidst plants not more than 6 inches high; the family is so numerous that probably other members of it will be found equally free-growing.

Knotweed, *Polygonum.*—Vigorous herbaceous plants, two at least very precious for our present aim, i. e. P. cuspidatum and P. sachalinense. These are among the plants that cannot be put in the garden without fear of their overrunning other things, while outside in the pleasure ground or plantation, or by the water-side where there is enough soil, they may be very handsome indeed. I find P. sachalinense is often very beautiful in foliage in the autumn when in the sun, and P. cuspidatum is most effective in flower in autumn. They are fine plants for deep soils and certainly can take care of themselves.

Pæony.—Vigorous herbaceous plants, with large and

THE GREAT JAPAN KNOTWEED (Polygonum cuspidatum).

splendid flowers of various shades of crimson, rosy-crimson, and white. There are many species and varieties, the flowers of some of the varieties being very sweet-scented, double, and among the largest flowers we have. Fringes of shrubberies, open glades in copses, and indeed almost any rough place, may be adorned by them ; and they may also be on the grass in the rougher parts of the pleasure ground. I never felt the beauty of the fine colour of Pæonies till

I saw a group of the double scarlet kind flowering in the long grass in Oxfordshire. The owner had placed a large group of this plant in an unmown glade, quite away from the garden proper ; and yet, seen from the lawn and garden, the effect was most brilliant. To be able to produce such effects in the early summer is a gain from a landscape point of view, apart from the beauty of the flowers when seen close at hand.

Poppy, *Papaver, in var.* – The huge and flaming Eastern Poppies, Papaver orientale, P. bracteatum, and P. lateritium, are the most important of this type. They will thrive and live long in almost any position, but the proper place for them is in open spots among strong herbaceous plants. For the wild garden the Welsh Poppy (Meconopsis cambrica) is one of the best plants. It is a cheerful plant at all seasons ; perched on some old dry wall its masses of foliage are very fresh, but when loaded with a profusion of large yellow blossoms the plant is handsome ; it is a determined colonizer, ready to hold its own anywhere. Its home is the wall, the rock, and the ruin. It even surpasses the Wallflower in adapting itself to out-of-the-way places ; it

PHLOMIS.—Type of handsome Labiates ; flowers admirably suited for the Wild Garden. (See p. 186.)

will spring up in the gravel walk under one's feet, and is happy among stones in the courtyard. It looks down on one from crevices in brick walls, from chinks where one could scarcely introduce a knife-blade, and it delights most in shady places. No plant can be better adapted for naturalizing on rough stony banks, old quarries, and gravel pits.

THE TALL OX-EYE DAISY
(Pyrethrum serotinum).

Phlomis.—Showy and stately herbaceous or half-shrubby plants, with a profusion of handsome yellow or purplish flowers. Excellent for naturalization in warm open woods, copses, banks, growing well in ordinary soil. Some kinds carpet the ground very closely and keep away weeds.

Virginian Poke, *Phytolacca decandra.*—A robust perennial, with long dense spikes of purplish berries. It will grow anywhere and in any soil; but is most imposing in rich deep ones. The berries are relished by birds, and it is fine for association with the stoutest herbaceous plants in rough places.

Lungwort, *Pulmonaria.* — Dwarf plants of the borage family, with showy blue or pinkish blossoms. Easily established in woods or copses, in which position the common blue one must be familiar to many in the woods of England and France. The plants are common in cottage gardens; they grow in any soil.

The tall Ox-eye Daisy, *Pyrethrum serotinum.*—This fine autumn flowering plant, for years left in the Botanic Gardens, is one of the handsomest flowers. It grows 5 or

6 feet high, and flowers late in autumn. It is picturesque in habit.

Bramble, *Rubus.*—Although we have nearly fifty kinds of bramble native in Britain, some of the exotic species, entirely distinct from our own, are well worthy of naturalization among low shrubs and tall herbaceous plants; for shady woods there is the large white Rubus Nutkanus, and the deep rose-coloured Rubus odoratus, and the early spring-flowering R. spectabilis; while the very striking white-stemmed R. biflorus is a good plant for warm slopes, sunny sides of chalk and gravel pits.

The Great Reed, *Arundo Donax.*—This noble reed I do not like to omit here, it is so beautiful in the southern counties of England, though in cold soils and hard winters it may perish. Where the hardier Bamboos find a place this will be welcome, though in our country it is only in the warmer parts that it attains the dignity it shows in the south of Europe.

Rhubarb, *Rheum.*—There are

THE GREAT REED of Southern Europe
(Arundo Donax).

several species of rhubarb in cultivation in addition to those commonly grown in gardens. They are much alike in port and in the size of their leaves, R. palmatum and Emodi being the most distinct. The rhubarbs are fine plants for association with large-leaved herbaceous plants in deep soils.

Rose, *Rosa.*—As in the case of brambles, we have many more kinds of wild roses in England than is commonly supposed, but nobody ever thinks of planting such things in gardens or shrubberies, where such ill-smelling and ugly things as privet make up the underwood. There are scores of the roses of northern and temperate countries which would thrive as well in our woodlands ; but as these are not to be obtained in our nurseries, it is useless to mention them. Any species of rose from a northern country might be tried ; whilst of roses commonly cultivated the climbing races—such as the Boursault, Ayrshire, and Sempervirens—are the most likely to be satisfactory. The Damask, Alba gallica, and vigorous climbers, being hardy, would do, as would Félicité-Perpétue, Banksiæflora, the Garland roses, Austrian brier, berberifolia, and microphylla rubra plena. Pruning, or any other attention after planting, should of course not be thought of in connexion with these. Rosa Brunoniana is a very fine free and hardy species from India. See the Chapter on Roses.

Sea Lavender, *Statice.*—Vigorous hardy plants with a profusion of bluish lavender-coloured bloom, thriving freely on all ordinary garden soils. S. latifolia, and some of the stronger kinds, thrive in any position.

Meadow Sweet, *Spiræa.*—Usually vigorous herbaceous plants, with white or rosy flowers. Such beautiful kinds as venusta and palmata are good among the medium-sized perennials. S. Aruncus is, perhaps, the finest plant for the wild garden. Mr. Ellam planted out some spare stock of S. japonica in a wood at Bodorgan, and with the happiest effect. The plants grow and flower freely, the flowers appearing a fortnight later in the moist cool wood than on plants of the same kind on a north garden border ; and so prolong the season of this favourite flower.

Golden Rod, *Solidago.*—Tall perennials with yellow flowers, showy when in bloom, and attractive when seen in America in autumn, mingled with the Starworts of that country, but rarely pretty as grown in gardens. These, like the worst of Asters, used to be grown to excess in the old borders ; but the positions they are best for are rough places, where in many cases it would be easy, with their aid and that of the Asters, to form that mixture of Golden Rod and Michaelmas Daisies which is one of the prettiest effects in American woods in autumn.

Catch-fly, *Silene.*—Dwarf or spreading plants, allied to the pinks, and generally with white or rosy flowers. The choice mountain kinds, such as S. Lagascæ, alpestris, Schafta, &c., are among the most charming subjects that can be naturalized on rocky places or banks, associated with very dwarf plants. Such fine annual or biennial kinds as S. Armeria or S. pendula are among the best, and might be easily established by scattering a few seeds in likely places.

Bloodwort, *Sanguinaria canadensis.*—This little plant, which abounds in the woods of Canada and North America, and which is very rarely indeed seen well grown in our gardens, will thrive under the branches of deciduous trees as well as the winter aconite, and in spring will give a beautiful effect.

Squill, *Scilla.*—Several kinds of Scilla, closely allied to the common bluebell, would do quite as well in our woods as that well-known native plant, notably S. campanulata, S. bifolia and S. sibirica. Bifolia and sibirica would be better on sunny banks or sheltered fringes of shrubberies. The tall kinds would do in woods or copses like the bluebell. With the dwarfer Scilla might be associated the grape hyacinth and the amethyst hyacinth (Hyacinthus amethystinus).

Comfrey, *Symphytum.*—Herbaceous plants of the borage order, usually with handsome blue flowers. One of the handsomest spring flowers is Symphytum caucasicum, and it is also one of the easiest things to naturalize, running about in shrubby places. Coarse kinds, like S. asperrimum (unfit for garden culture), thrive apace among the largest plants in ditches and rich bottoms, and look beautiful when in flower.

Scabious, *Scabiosa, Cephalaria, Knautia.*—Sometimes handsome and free-growing herbaceous plants, bluish, purplish, or yellowish in colour of flowers. Among these may be seen, in botanic and other gardens, plants suited for naturalization, but scarcely worthy of a place in the garden. The fine S. caucasica would thrive in warm soil, as would the Knautias in any soil.

Stonecrop, *Sedum.*—Small and usually prostrate plants, with white, yellow, or rosy flowers, and occurring in multitudes on most of the mountain chains of northern and temperate countries. There are few of these pretty plants that would not grow on the top of an old wall, or thatched house, or stony bank, or bare ground, as well as our common Stonecrop. All grow in any soil, are as easily increased as any weed, and grow anywhere if they are not too much overshadowed by trees and coarser vegetation. Such kinds as S. spurium, S. pulchellum, kamtschaticum, and S. spectabile are among the best.

Rockfoil, *Saxifraga.*—A very extensive family of plants, abundant on mountains in northern countries. For our purpose they may be thrown into five sections—the mossy section, represented in Britain by S. hypnoides; the silvery section, represented by S. Aizoon; the London Pride section, by the Kerry saxifrages; the Megasea section, by the large S. crassifolia; and the oppositifolia section, distinguished by its rosy-purple flowers. With the exception of the Megasea and oppositifolia sections, which have rosy flowers, most of the saxifrages have white blossoms spotted with red; a few are yellow, and all are very hardy, and the easiest to grow of all alpine flowers. The mossy, silvery, and purple saxifrages may be naturalized with the greatest ease on bare rocky or mountainous grounds, amidst dwarf vegetation; but, as the places in which this kind of ground occurs are comparatively few, the Megaseas and the Kerry saxifrages are probably the most generally useful, as they can fight their way amongst grass and other common herbs. There are probably nearly 150 species in cultivation in England.

Houseleek, *Sempervivum.*—Very dwarf and succulent plants, with their fleshy leaves arranged in dense rosettes, and mostly with curious but seldom conspicuous flowers. They abound in mountainous regions, and are very hardy. The greater number of these grow quite as freely as the common Houseleek in any arid soil, and in any position where the vegetation is not taller than themselves, such as on bare sandy banks, gravelly heaps, &c. There are about fifty hardy kinds in cultivation in this country.

Meadow Rue, *Thalictrum.*—Tall herbaceous plants, often affording a pleasing effect when seen in groups, and hence pretty for this mode of gardening. They grow in any soil, and should be placed among rank vegetation. There are many kinds not differing much in aspect; some of the smaller ones, like our British T. minus, deserve a place among dwarf plants for the elegance of their leaves. With these last may be associated the Italian Isopyrum thalictroides, which is handsome in flower and leaf.

Spiderwort, *Tradescantia virginica.*—A handsome North American perennial, with purple, blue, or white flowers, attaining a height of 1½ feet or 2 feet. A good plant for naturalization on almost any soil, thriving often on the wettest, and therefore suited for many places where other perennials would make little progress.

TELEKIA.   Type of the larger Composites, excluded from gardens proper.

Wood Lily, *Trillium.*—Very singular and beautiful American wood plants, of which T. grandiflorum is worthy of special mention, thriving in shady places in moist rich soils, in woods and copses, where some vegetable soil has gathered.

Globe Flower, *Trollius.*—Beautiful plants of vigorous habit, with handsome yellow flowers, of a fine colour, like those of the buttercups, but turning inwards so as to form an almost round blossom, quite distinct in aspect. Few plants are more worthy of a position in grassy glades where the soil is rich, although they will grow in ordinary soil. There are several distinct kinds suitable, though there is little difference in their effect. I have established them without trouble in wettish places foul with crowfoot and other bad weeds, and planting them without any preparation of the ground.

Tulip, *Tulipa.*—Various species of Tulips might be naturalized by wood walks and in the rougher parts of the pleasure
grounds. In such positions they would not attain such a size
as the richly-fed garden flowers, but that would make them
none the less attractive to those who care about the wild
garden.

Telekia, *Telekia cordifolia.*—A vigorous herbaceous plant,
suited for association with Echinops, Rheum, and plants

Group of TRITOMA, in grass (by Lake Longleat).

grown for their foliage. It is very free in growth, and has
large leaves and sunflower-like flowers.

Flame-Flower, *Tritoma.*—Flame-Flowers are occasionally
planted in excess, so as to neutralize the good effect they
might otherwise produce, and they, like many other flowers,
have suffered from being, like soldiers, put in straight lines
and in other geometrical formations. It is only where a fine
plant or group of plants is seen in some green glade that
the true beauty of the Flame-Flower is seen. Although not

always hardy plants, they are so free in many soils that they might with confidence be planted in the wild garden, and our sketch shows a picturesque group of them planted in this way.

Showy Indian Cress, *Tropæolum speciosum.*—Against walls, among shrubs, and on slopes, on moist banks, or bushy banks near the hardy fernery, in deep, rich, and light soil, this brilliant plant is well worth any trouble to establish. Many fail with it in the garden, but moist, shady, and bushy places will suit it better, and, in the south of England and on warm soils. the north sides of houses and walls, rocks and beds of shrubs should be chosen.

Mullein, *Verbascum.*—Verbascum vernale is a noble plant, which has been slowly spreading in our collections of hardy plants for some years past, and it is one of peculiar merit. I first saw it in the Garden of Plants, and brought home some roots which gave rise to the stock now in our gardens. Its peculiarity, or rather its merit, is that it is a true perennial species—at least on warm soils—and in this respect quite unlike other Mulleins that are sometimes seen in our gardens, and oftener in our hedgerows. It also has the advantage of great height, growing to a height of 10 feet, or even more. Then there are the large and green leaves, which come up rather early and are extremely effective. Finally, the colour is good and the quantity of yellow flowers with purplish filaments that are borne on one of these great branching panicles is enormous. The use of such a plant cannot be difficult to define, it being so good in form and so distinct in habit. Another good kind is V. phlomoides, which I saw last autumn abundantly wild in Touraine, in stony places about Chenonceau, and which might be sown with us in like places.

Periwinkle, *Vinca.*—Trailing plants, with glossy foliage and blue flowers, well known in gardens. They grow in any position, shady or sunny. There are variously-coloured and very pretty varieties of V. minor, while the variegated forms of both species are pretty.

Speedwell, *Veronica.* — Herbaceous and alpine plants, usually rather tall (1½ feet to 3 feet), in some cases dwarf alpine plants with blue flowers in various shades; they are among the hardiest of plants, and will grow in any soil. All the taller kinds are admirably suited for naturalization among long grass and other herbaceous vegetation. Very many that are in cultivation in borders are fit only for the wild garden. The dwarf kinds are equally suitable for bare places, or among other dwarf plants.

Violet, *Viola.* — A numerous race of dwarf and interesting plants, thriving freely in our climate, in half-shady places, rocky spots or banks, fringes of

TALL MULLEIN.

shrubberies, or almost any position. The very handsome bird's-foot Violet of North America (V. pedata) would thrive in sandy level places or on rocky banks. In this family occur a good many kinds, such as V. canadensis, which,

not being fragrant, or not possessing sufficient charms to
ensure their general cultivation in gardens, are best suited
for wild gardening. Our own sweet Violet should be
abundantly planted wherever it does not occur in a wild
state.

LARGE WHITE ACHILLEAS, spread into wide masses under shade of trees in shrubbery.

CHAPTER XV.

OPHRYS in grass.

AN important point is the getting of a stock of plants to begin with. In country or other places where many good old borderflowers remain in the cottage gardens, many plants may be found. Nursery beds should be formed in which such plants could be increased. Free-growing spring-flowers, like Aubrietia, Alyssum, and Iberis, may be multiplied to any extent by division or cuttings. Numbers of kinds may be raised from seed sown rather thinly in drills, in nursery beds in the open air. The best time for sowing is spring, but any time in summer will do. Many perennials and bulbs must be bought in nurseries, and increased as well as may be in nursery beds. As to soil, the best way is to avoid the trouble of preparing it; the point is to adapt the plant to the soil—in peaty places to place plants that thrive in peat, in clay soils those that thrive in clays, and so on.

A Selection of Plants for Naturalization in places with dwarf vegetation, on bare banks, and in poorish soil.

Dielytra eximia.
,, formosa.
Arabis albida.
Aubrietia, in var.
Alyssum saxatile.
Iberis corifolia.
,, sempervirens.
,, correæfolia.
Thlaspi latifolium.
Helianthemum, in var.
Viola cornuta.
,, cucullata.
Gypsophila repens.
Tunica Saxifraga.
Saponaria ocymoides.
Silene alpestris.
,, Schafta.
Cerastium Biebersteinii.
,, grandiflorum.
,, tomentosum.
Linum alpinum.
,, arboreum.
,, flavum.
Geranium Wallichianum.
,, striatum.
,, cinereum, and others.
Oxalis floribunda.
Genista sagittalis.
Anthyllis montana.
Astragalus monspessulanus.
Coronilla varia.
Hedysarum obscurum.
Vicia argentea.
Orobus vernus.
,, lathyroides.

Waldsteinia trifolia.
Potentilla.
Œnothera speciosa.
,, missouriensis.
,, taraxacifolia.
Sedum dentatum.
,, kamtschaticum.
,, Sieboldii.
,, spectabile.
,, spurium.
Sempervivum calcareum.
,, hirtum.
,, montanum.
,, soboliferum.
,, sedoides.
Saxifraga Aizoon.
,, cordifolia.
,, crassifolia.
,, crustata.
,, longifolia.
,, Cotyledon.
,, rosularis.
Astrantia major.
Dondia Epipactis.
Athamanta Matthioli.
Cornus canadensis.
Scabiosa caucasica.
Hieracium aurantiacum.
Doronicum caucasicum.
Aster alpinus.
Tussilago fragrans.
Achillea aurea.
Symphyandra pendula.
Campanula carpatica.
,, fragilis.
,, garganica.
,, cæspitosa.

Vinca herbacea.
Gentiana acaulis.
Phlox stolonifera.
,, subulata.
,, amœna.
Lithospermum prostratum.
Pulmonaria grandiflora.
,, mollis.
Myosotis dissitiflora.
Physalis Alkekengi.
Pentstemon procerus.
Veronica austriaca.
,, candida.
,, taurica, and many others.
Teucrium Chamædrys.
Ajuga genevensis.
Scutellaria alpina.
Prunella grandiflora.
Stachys lanata.
Zietenia lavandulæfolia.
Dodecatheon Meadia.
Acantholimon glumaceum.
Armeria cephalotes.
Plumbago Larpentæ.
Polygonum Brunonis.
,, vaccinifolium.
Euphorbia Cyparissias.
Iris cristata.
,, graminea.
,, pumila.
,, reticulata.
,, nudicaulis, and many others.

Plants of vigorous habit for the Wild Garden.

Trollius, any kind.
Thalictrum aquilegifolium.
Delphinium, in var.
Aconitum, in var.
Pæonia, in var.

Papaver orientale.
,, bracteatum.
Macleaya cordata.
Datisca cannabina.
Crambe cordifolia.
Althæa ficifolia.

Althæa nudiflora.
,, taurinensis.
Lavatera Olbia.
Galega officinalis.
,, biloba.
Lathyrus latifolius.

Lathyrus grandiflorus, and any others.
Lupinus polyphyllus.
Thermopsis barbata.
Spiræa Aruncus.
Astilbe rivularis & rubra.
Molopospermum cicutarium.
Ferula communis.
,, glauca.
,, tingitana.
,, sulcata.
Statice latifolia.
Peucedanum involucratum.
,, longifolium.
Heracleum, any exotic kinds.
Dipsacus laciniatus.
Mulgedium Plumieri.
Alfredia cernua.

Onopordon, any.
Centaurea babylonica.
Echinops bannaticus.
,, exaltatus.
,, ruthenicus.
,, purpureus.
Aster elegans.
,, Novi Belgii.
,, Novæ Angliæ.
,, ericoides, and any strong and pretty kinds.
Eupatorium purpureum.
Telekia cordifolia.
Helianthus angustifolius.
,, multiflorus.
,, orgyalis and others.
Harpalium rigidum.
Silphium perfoliatum.
Campanula, all the tall and showy kinds.

Asclepias Cornuti.
,, Douglasii.
Verbascum Chaixii.
,, phlomoides.
Physostegia imbricata.
,, speciosa.
Acanthus latifolius.
,, spinosus.
,, spinosissimus.
Phytolacca decandra.
Polygonum Sieboldii.
,, sachalinense.
Rheum Emodi.
,, palmatum.
Achillea Eupatorium.
Bambusa, hardiest kinds.
Veratrum album.
Yucca flaccida
,, recurva.
Peucedanum ruthenicum.
Astragalus ponticus.

Hardy Plants with fine foliage or graceful habit suitable for Naturalization.

Acanthus, several species.
Asclepias syriaca.
Statice latifolia.
Polygonum cuspidatum.
,, sachalinense.
Rheum Emodi, and other kinds.
Euphorbia Cyparissias.
Datisca cannabina.
Veratrum album.
Crambe cordifolia.
Althæa taurinensis.
Elymus arenarius.
Bambusa, several species.
Arundinaria falcata.

Yucca, several species.
Verbascum Chaixii.
Spiræa Aruncus.
Astilbe rivularis.
,, rubra.
Eryngium, several species.
Ferula, several species.
Phytolacca decandra.
Centaurea babylonica.
Actæa, in var.
Cimicifuga racemosa.
Heracleum, several species.
Aralia japonica.
,, edulis.
Macleaya cordata.

Panicum bulbosum.
,, virgatum.
Dipsacus laciniatus.
Alfredia cernua.
Carlina acanthifolia.
Telekia cordifolia.
Echinops exaltatus.
,, ruthenicus.
Helianthus orgyalis, and others.
Silybum eburneum.
,, Marianum.
Onopordon Acanthium.
,, arabicum.
,, tauricum.

Plants for Hedge-banks and like Places.

Aster, in variety.
Clematis, the wild species, in var.
Thalictrum aquilegifolium.

Anemone japonica, and vars.
Delphinium, in var.
Chrysanthemum maximum, and allied kinds.

Aconitum, in var.
Macleaya cordata.
Kitaibelia vitifolia.
Tropæolum speciosum.
Baptisia australis.

Coronilla varia.
Galega officinalis, both white and pink forms.
Galega biloba.
Astragalus ponticus.
Lathyrus grandiflorus.
,, rotundifolius.
,, latifolius.
,, ,, albus.
Rubus biflorus.
Œnothera Lamarckiana.

Astilbe rivularis.
Ferula, in var.
Campanula, in great var.
Calystegia dahurica.
,, pubescens.
Verbascum Chaixii.
Veronica,tall kinds in var.
Phlomis Russelliana.
,, Herba-venti.
Physostegia speciosa.
,, virginica.

Lilies, common kinds.
Narcissus, common kinds.
Scillas, in var.
Phytolacca decandra.
Aristolochia Sipho.
Asparagus Broussoneti.
,, officinalis.
Vitis, in var.
Honeysuckles, in var.
Leucojum, in var.
Fritillary, in var.

Trailers and Climbers.

The selection of plants to cover banks and old trees suitably is important, particularly as the plants fitted for these purposes are equally useful for rocks, precipitous banks, sides of bridges, river-banks, ruins, covering out-houses, or rough sheds in pastures.

Vitis æstivalis.
., amoorensis.
,, cordifolia.
,, Isabella.
., Labrusca.
,, laciniosa.
,, riparia.
,, Sieboldii.
,, vulpina.
Aristolochia Sipho.
,, tomentosa.

Clematis, in variety, species.
Calystegia dahurica.
Wistaria sinensis.
Periploca græca.
Hablitzia tamnoides
Boussingaultia basel-loides.
Menispermum cana-dense.
,, virginicum.

Cissus orientalis.
,, pubescens.
Ampelopsis bipinnata.
,, cordata.
,, hederacea.
,, tricuspidata.
Jasminum nudiflorum.
,, officinale.
,, revolutum.
Passiflora cœrulea.
Lonicera, in variety.

Spring and early Summer Flowers for Naturalization.

Anemone alpina.
,, apennina.
,, blanda.
,, coronaria.
,, fulgens.
,, Hepatica.
,, ranunculoides.
,, trifolia, and many others.
Ranunculus aconitifolius.
,, amplexicaulis.
,, montanus.

Helleborus niger.
,, olympicus and many other kinds.
Eranthis hyemalis.
Aquilegia, various.
Pæonia, many kinds.
Epimedium pinnatum.
Papaver bracteatum.
,, orientale.
Dielytra eximia.
,, spectabilis.

Corydalis capnoides.
,, lutea.
Arabis.
Aubrietia, various.
Alyssum saxatile.
Iberis corifolia.
,, sempervirens.
., correæfolia.
Viola cornuta.
Saponaria ocymoides.
Silene alpestris.
Arenaria montana.

Vicia argentea.
Orobus flaccidus.
,, cyaneus.
,, lathyroides.
,, variegatus.
,, vernus.
Centaurea montana.
Doronicum caucasicum.
Thlaspi latifolium, and others.
Hesperis matronalis.
Erica carnea.
Vinca major.
Gentiana acaulis.
Phlox reptans, and other alpine Phlox.
Pulmonaria grandiflora.
,, mollis.
Symphytum bohemicum.
,, caucasicum.
Myosotis dissitiflora.
Omphalodes verna.
Dodecatheon Jeffreyi.
,, Meadia.
Cyclamen europæum.
,, hederæfolium.

Primula, in var.
Iris amœna.
,, cristata.
,, De Bergii.
,, flavescens.
,, florentina.
,, germanica.
,, graminea.
,, ochroleuca.
,, pallida.
,, sambucina.
,, sub-biflora, and many other kinds.
Crocus aureus.
,, speciosus.
,, versicolor.
,, susianus, and many others.
Narcissus angustifolius.
,, bicolor.
,, incomparabilis.
,, major.
,, montanus.
,, odorus.
,, poeticus & vars.
(All the hardy kinds are

fitted for the wild garden.)
Galanthus, in var.
Leucojum pulchellum.
,, vernum.
Paradisia Liliastrum.
Ornithogalum, various.
Scilla amœna.
,, bifolia.
,, altaica.
,, campanulata.
,, italica.
,, sibirica.
Hyacinthus amethystinus.
Muscari botryoides.
,, moschatum, and various others.
Allium neapolitanum.
,, ciliatum.
Tulipa Gesneriana.
,, suaveolens.
,, scabriscapa, and many others.
Fritillaria, in var.
Bulbocodium vernum.

Plants for Naturalization beneath Trees on Lawns.

Where the branches of trees, both evergreen and deciduous, sweep the turf, a great number of pretty spring flowers may be naturalized beneath the branches, where they will thrive without attention. It is chiefly in the case of deciduous trees that this could be done ; but even in the case of conifers and evergreens some graceful little spring flowers might be dotted beneath the outermost points of their lower branches. We know that many of our spring flowers and hardy bulbs mature their leaves and go to rest early in the year. They enjoy the sun in spring, under the deciduous tree ; they have time to flower and develop their leaves under it before the foliage of the tree appears ; then, as the summer comes, they are gradually overshadowed and go to rest ; the leaves of the trees once fallen, they soon begin to appear again and cover the ground with beauty.

Take a spreading old summer-leafing tree, and scatter a few tufts of the winter Aconite beneath it, and leave them alone. In a very few years they will have covered the ground; every year afterwards they will spread a pretty carpet beneath the tree ; and when the carpet fades there will be no eyesore from decaying leaves as there would be on a border — no need to replace the plants with others ; the tree puts forth its leaves, covering the ground till autumn, and in early spring we again see our little friend in his glossy coat and yellow buttons. There are other plants of which the same is true. We have only to imagine this done in a variety of cases to see to what a beautiful result it would lead. Given the bright blue Apennine Anemone under one tree, the spring Snowflake under another, the bright and many coloured Crocuses, and so on, we should have a spring garden of the most beautiful kind. The plan could be carried out under the branches of a grove as well as under those of specimen trees. Pretty mixed plantations might be made by dotting tall plants, like the large Jonquil and other Narcissus, among dwarf spreading plants like the blue Anemone. The following are selected as among the most suitable for such arrangements as that just described, with some little attention as to the season of flowering and the kind of soil required by some rather uncommon species. A late-flowering kind, for example, should be planted under late-leafing trees, or towards the points of their branches, so that they might not be obscured by the leaves of the tree before perfecting their flowers.

Anemone angulosa.	Anemone blanda.	Anemone fulgens.
,, apennina.	,, Coronaria.	,, Hepatica.

Anemone stellata.
„ sylvestris.
„ trifolia.
Arum italicum.
Bulbocodium vernum.
Corydalis, solida.
„ tuberosa.
Crocus Imperati.
„ biflorus.
„ reticulatus.

Crocus versicolor, and many others.
Cyclamen in variety.
Eranthis hyemalis.
Erythronium Dens-canis.
Ficaria grandiflora.
Snowdrop, many kinds.
Snowflake, all the kinds.
Iris reticulata.

Muscari, any of the numerous kinds.
Narcissus, in var.
Puschkinia scilloides.
Sanguinaria canadensis.
Scilla bifolia.
„ sibirica.
„ campanulata.
Trillium grandiflorum.
Tulipa, species in var.

Plants for very moist rich Soils.

Althæa, in var.
Astilbe rivularis.
Aralia edulis.
„ nudicaulis.
Asclepias Cornuti.
Asphodelus ramosus.
Aster, in var.
Baptisia exaltata.
Caltha palustris fl. pl.
Campanula glomerata, and large kinds.
Convallaria multiflora.
Colchicum, in var.
Crinum capense.
Datisca cannabina.
Echinops, in var.
Elymus, in var.
Epilobium, in var.
Eupatorium, in var.

Galax aphylla.
Galega officinalis.
Gentiana asclepiadea.
Helianthus multiflorus.
„ orgyalis.
„ rigidus.
Helonias bullata.
Hemerocallis, in var.
Heracleum, in var.
Iris ochroleuca.
Liatris, in var.
Lythrum roseum superbum.
Mimulus, in var.
Mulgedium Plumieri.
Narcissus, stronger kinds.
Œnothera, large kinds.
Onopordon, in var.
Phlomis Herba-venti.

Phlomis Russelliana.
Physostegia speciosa.
Phytolacca decandra.
Rudbeckia, in var.
Ranunculus amplexicaulis.
„ parnassifolius.
Sanguinaria canadensis.
Solidago, in var.
Spiræa Aruncus.
Silphium, in var.
Swertia perennis.
Telekia speciosa.
Thalictrum, in var.
Trollius, in var.
Vaccinium, in var.
Veratrum, in var.
Polygonum, in var.

Plants suited for Peat Soil.

Alstrœmeria, in var.
Calluna, in var.
Chimaphila maculata.
Chrysobactron Hookeri.
Coptis trifoliata.
Cornus canadensis.
Cypripedium spectabile.
Dentaria laciniata.
Daphne Cneorum.
Dryas octopetala.
Epigæa repens.
Epimedium, in var.

Funkia Sieboldii.
„ grandiflora.
Galax aphylla.
Gaultheria procumbens.
Gentians, in var.
Helonias bullata.
Iris nudicaulis, pumila, and vars.
Jeffersonia diphylla.
Linnæa borealis.
Podophyllum peltatum.
„ Emodi.

Polygala Chamæbuxus.
Pyrola, in var.
Hardy Heaths, in var.
Ramondia pyrenaica.
Sisyrinchium grandiflorum.
Spigelia marilandica.
Trientalis europæa.
Trillium grandiflorum.
Lilies, in var.

Plants suited for Calcareous Soil.

Adenophora, in var.
Æthionema, in var.
Anemone, in var.
Alyssum, in var.
Anthyllis montana.
Antirrhinum, in var.
Cistus, in var.
Cheiranthus, in var.
Campanula, in var.
Carduus eriophorus.
Coronilla, in var.
Dianthus, in var.
Echium, in var.
Erodium, in var.
Genista, in var.
Geum, in var.

Geranium, in var.
Gypsophila, in var.
Hedysarum, in var.
Helianthemum, in var.
Lunaria biennis.
Onobrychis, in var.
Ononis, in var.
Ophrys, in var.
Othonna cheirifolia.
Phlomis, in var.
Prunella grandiflora.
Santolina, in var.
Saponaria ocymoides.
Saxifraga (the encrusted and the large-leaved kinds).

Scabiosa, in var.
Sempervivum, in var.
Sedum, in var.
Symphytum, in var.
Thermopsis fabacea.
Thymus, in var.
Trachelium cœruleum.
Trifolium alpinum.
Triteleia uniflora.
Tunica Saxifraga.
Vesicaria utriculata.
Vicia, in var.
Vittadenia, triloba.
Waldsteinia trifoliata.
   ,,   geoides.

Plants suited for Dry and Gravelly Soil.

Achillæa, in var.
Æthionema cordifolium.
Agrostemma coronaria.
Alyssum saxatile.
Antennaria dioica.
Anthyllis montana.
Antirrhinum rupestre.
Arabis albida.
Aubrietia, in var.
Armeria cephalotes.
Artemisia, in var.
Cerastium, in var.
Carlina acanthifolia.
Cheiranthus, in var.
Chrysopsis Mariana.
Cistus, in var.
Corydalis, in var.
Dianthus, in var.
Dracocephalum, in var.
Dielytra eximia.

Dorycnium sericeum.
Echium, in var.
Erodium, in var.
Eryngium, in var.
Euphorbia Myrsinites.
Fumaria, in var.
Geranium, in var.
Gypsophila, in var.
Helianthemum, in var.
Helichrysum arenarium.
Hypericum, in var.
Iberis, in var.
Jasione perennis.
Lavandula Spica.
Linaria, in var.
Linum, in var.
Lupinus polyphyllus.
Modiola geranioides.
Nepeta Mussinii.
Onobrychis, in var.

Ononis, in var.
Ornithogalum, in var.
Plumbago Larpentæ.
Polygonum vaccinifolium.
Santolina, in var.
Scabiosa, in var.
Sedum, in great var.
Sempervivum, in great var.
Saponaria ocymoides.
Stachys lanata.
Teucrium Chamædrys.
Thlaspi latifolium.
Thymus, in var.
Trachelium, in var.
Tussilago fragrans.
Verbascum, in var.
Vesicaria utriculata.
Rosmary.

Selection of Plants for Growing on Old Walls, Ruins, or Rocky Slopes.

Achillea tomentosa.
Alyssum montanum.
   ,,   saxatile.

Antirrhinum rupestre.
   ,,   majus.
   ,,   Orontium.

Arenaria balearica.
   ,,   cæspitosa.
   ,,   ciliata.

Arenaria graminifolia.
„ montana.
„ verna.
Arabis albida.
„ petræa.
Asperula cynanchica.
Campanula Barrelieri.
„ rotundifolia.
„ fragilis.
„ fragilis lanuginosa.
„ garganica.
„ pumila.
„ pumila alba.
Centranthus ruber.
„ albus.
„ coccineus.
Cheiranthus alpinus.
„ Cheiri.
„ „ pleno.
Coronilla minima.
Corydalis lutea.
Cotyledon Umbilicus.
Dianthus cæsius.
„ deltoides.
„ monspessulanus.
„ petræus.
Draba aizoides.
Erinus alpinus.
Erodium romanum.
„ Reichardii.
Gypsophila muralis.
„ prostrata.
Helianthemum, in var.
Hutchinsia petræa.

Iberis, in var.
Ionopsidium acaule.
Königa maritima.
Linum alpinum.
Lychnis alpina.
„ Flos-Jovis.
„ lapponica.
Malva campanulata.
Santolina lanata.
Saponaria ocymoides.
Saxifraga bryoides.
„ caryophyllata.
„ cæsia.
„ crustata.
„ cuscutæformis.
„ diapensioides.
„ Hostii.
„ intacta.
„ ligulata.
„ longifolia.
„ pectinata.
„ pulchella.
„ retusa.
„ Rhei.
„ rosularis.
„ Rocheliana.
„ sarmentosa.
Sedum acre.
„ aureum.
„ Aizoon.
„ album.
„ anglicum.
„ arenarium.
„ brevifolium.
„ californicum.

Sedum cœruleum.
„ dasyphyllum.
„ elegans.
„ Ewersii.
„ farinosum.
„ globiferum.
„ Heuffelli.
„ hirtum.
„ hispanicum.
„ kamschaticum.
„ montanum.
„ multiceps.
„ piliferum.
„ pulchrum.
„ sempervivoides.
Sempervivum arachnoideum.
„ soboliferum.
„ spurium.
„ sexangulare.
„ sexfidum.
„ tectorum.
Silene alpestris.
„ rupestris.
„ Schafta.
Symphyandra pendula.
Thlaspi alpestre.
Thymus citriodorus.
Trichomanes, and vars.
Tunica Saxifraga.
Umbilicus chrysanthus.
Veronica fruticulosa.
„ saxatilis.
Vesicaria utriculata.

A Selection of Annual and Biennial Plants for Naturalization.

Papaver somniferum.
Eschscholtzia californica.
Platystemon californicum.
Matthiola annua.
„ bicornis.
Arabis arenosa.
Alyssum maritimum.
Iberis coronaria.
„ umbellata.

Malcolmia maritima.
Erysimum Peroffskianum.
Gypsophila elegans.
Saponaria calabrica.
Silene Armeria.
Viscaria oculata.
Malope trifida.
Limnanthes Douglasii.
Ononis viscosa.
Œnothera odorata.

Godetia, various.
Clarkia elegans.
„ pulchella.
Amberboa moschata.
„ odorata.
Dimorphotheca pluvia.
Gilia capitata.
„ tricolor.
Collomia coccinea.
Leptosiphon androsaceus.

Leptosiphon densiflorus.	Bromus brizæformis.	Œnothera Jamesi.
Nicandra physaloides.	Briza, in var.	Œnothera Lamarckiana.
Collinsia bicolor.	Agrostis nebulosa.	Dipsacus laciniatus.
„　verna.	Matthiola, in var.	Silybum eburneum.
Dracocephalum nutans.	Lunaria biennis.	Onopordon, in var.
„　moldavicum.	Hesperis matronalis.	Campanula Medium and
Blitum capitatum.	Erysimum asperum.	vars.
Polygonum orientale.	Silene pendula.	Verbascum phlomoides.
Panicum capillare.	Hedysarum coronarium.	

Grasses for Naturalization.

Agrostis nebulosa.	Hordeum jubatum.	Polypogon monspeliensis.
Briza maxima.	Panicum virgatum.	Stipa gigantea.
Brizopyrum siculum.	„　bulbosum.	„　pennata.
Bromus brizæformis.	„　capillare.	Milium multiflorum.

Some of our nobler grasses, like the Pampas and the New Zealand reeds, have not the qualities of perfect hardiness and power of increase without care in our climate that would entitle them to a place in these selections.

Hardy Bulbs for Naturalization.

Allium Moly.	Cyclamen, in var.	Muscari, in var.
„　fragrans.	Erythronium, in var.	Narcissus, in great var.
„　neapolitanum.	Fritillaria, in var.	Ornithogalum, in var.
„　ciliatum.	Gladiolus, hardy Euro-	Scilla, in var.
Brodiæa congesta.	pean species.	Snowdrops, in var.
Bulbocodium vernum.	Hyacinthus amethystinus.	Sternbergia lutea.
Camassia esculenta.	Leucojum, in var.	Trichonema ramiflorum.
Crocus, in great var.	Lilium, in var.	Triteleia uniflora.
Colchicum, in var.	Merendera Bulbocodium.	Tulipa, in var.

List of Plants for Naturalization in Lawns and other Grassy Places.

Bulbocodium vernum.	Scilla italica.	Dianthus deltoides.
Colchicum, in var.	„　amœna.	Fumaria bulbosa.
Crocus, many.	Anemone apennina.	Narcissus, many kinds.
Snowdrops, all.	„　ranunculoides.	Hyacinthus amethystinus.
Leucojum, various.	„　blanda.	Merendera Bulbocodium.
Scilla bifolia.	„　trifolia.	Muscari, in var.
„　alba.	Antennaria dioica rosea.	Trichonema ramiflorum.
„　sibirica.	Anthyllis montana.	

Climbing and Twining Plants for Thickets, Hedgerows, and Trees.

Ampelopsis bipinnata.	Clematis Viticella, and others.	Menispermum canadense.
,, cordata.	Hablitzia tamnoides.	,, virginicum.
,, hederacea.	Jasminum nudiflorum.	Periploca græca.
,, tricuspidata.	,, officinale.	Roses, single, in great var.
Apios tuberosa.	Lathyrus grandiflorus.	Smilax, hardy kinds.
Aristolochia Sipho.	,, latifolius.	Tamus communis.
,, tomentosa.	,, rotundifolius.	Tropæolum pentaphyllum.
Calystegia dahurica.	,, tuberosus and others.	,, speciosum.
Cissus orientalis.		Vitis, various.
Clematis flammula.	Lonicera, in variety.	Wistaria frutescens.
,, montana.		,, sinensis.

These selections are proposed only as aids to those dealing with special positions. The selection and best guide to the material for the beginner will be found in the Chapter on the principal types of Hardy Exotic Plants for the wild garden.

RABBITS.

This sad subject has been kept for the last, as the only disagreeable one in connexion with the wild garden.

It is incalculable the injury rabbits do to young trees alone ; indeed, where they prevail there is no chance of getting up cover except at an extravagant cost. Hares are less destructive, if they damage trees at all ; and it is said by experienced gamekeepers that they never thrive so well where rabbits abound. And as regards pheasants, rabbits drive them away by eating down the evergreen cover so necessary for shelter in winter. Pheasants will not remain in a wood where there is not shelter of this kind ; and nothing are they more partial to than the Holly, which ought to abound in every wood, but which the rabbits destroy first. Here are two sorts of game—hares and pheasants—which many can never have enough of, and the existence of which is directly interfered with by the rabbits ; not to speak of the expense incurred year after year making up losses in plantation, and the expense of wire-netting in protecting the trees. The extermination of rabbits is not such a difficult matter as might be imagined. When it was determined here a few years since to reduce their numbers to a minimum on the farm lands and woods, it did not require more than a couple of years to do so by shooting and ferreting during the season ; and they are now principally confined to one part of the estate—an extensive tract of waste land not of much use for any other purpose. I feel pretty certain that a few active poachers would undertake to clear an estate of its rabbits in a short time, and would be glad to pay for the right of doing so. In whatever degree rabbits contribute to our food supply—and it is not much —they certainly destroy a great quantity of our crops, are no profit to game preservers, and there is little excuse for their existence.

Hungry rabbits, like hungry dogs or starving men, will eat almost anything that can be got. Rabbits, as a rule, prefer to nibble over a pasture that contains short, sweet, wholesome grass, and a proportion of Clover, Dandelion, and Daisies ; but in and about woods where rabbits are numerous, the grass, from being closely and constantly eaten off, gradually disappears, and at the approach of winter is succeeded by Moss, a very cold, watery, and innutritious substitute ; then rabbits are driven to seek food from other sources than grass, and the bark of small trees, the leaves, stalks, and bark of shrubs, are eaten almost indiscriminately. Amongst evergreen shrubs, Rhododendrons and Box are generally avoided, but I have known newly-planted Rhododendrons to be eaten by rabbits. The elder is distasteful, and American Azaleas are avoided. I have frequently seen Yew trees barked ; Mahonias are devoured in these woods as soon as planted ; and Periwinkle, which is named amongst rabbit-proof plants, is generally eaten to the ground in severe weather. Where rabbits are permitted, the fact that they require food daily, like other creatures, should be recognized. A certain portion of grass land should be retained for them and managed for them ; a few acres might be wired round, or, surrounded with wire-netting, to the exclusion of rabbits, until the approach of wintry weather, when it could be thrown open for them. If this cannot be done, and frosty weather sets in, when the mischief to shrubs is done, trimmings of quick hedges should be scattered about, and an allowance of turnips, carrots, or mangold wurzel made and doled out daily in bad weather. Rabbits prefer newly-planted trees and shrubs to those established. I have even had the fronds of newly-planted Athyrium Filix-fœmina eaten, while other ferns have been untouched : certain breeds of wild rabbits are much more prone to bark trees than others. The barking of trees is more done by north-country rabbits.—J. S.

A correspondent who has given much attention to the subject (Salmoniceps) gives the following, as among the most rabbit-proof of plants :—' Most of the Lily family are,' he says, ' rejected by them, including Daffodils, Tulips, Snowdrops, Snowflakes, Lilies, Day Lilies, Asphodels, and others, and they cannot be too extensively planted ; but even in that tribe the Crocus is greedily devoured.'

Androsæmum officinale.	Cineraria maritima.	Honesty (Lunaria).
Anemone coronaria.	Columbine.	Iris.
,, japonica.	Common Yews.	Lilies (common orange
Arabis.	Deutzia scabra.	and white kinds).
Artemisia Abrotanum.	Dog's-tooth Violet.	Lily of the Valley.
Asphodelus albus.	Elder.	Lonicera, in var.
Aubrietia.	Euonymus.	Lycium barbarum.
Berberis Darwinii.	Fuchsia.	Mahonia Aquifolium.
Canterbury Bells.	Hibiscus syriacus.	Monkshood.

Muscari.	Primrose.	Syringa vulgaris.
Narcissus.	Ruscus aculeatus.	Tritoma.
Ornithogalum.	„ racemosus.	Violets.
Pansies.	Scilla.	Weigela rosea.
Periwinkle (large and small).	Snowberry.	Winter Aconite.
Phlox, in var.	Solomon's Seal.	Woodruff.
Poppy.	Stachys lanata.	Yucca gloriosa.
	Syringa persica.	

Lists, however, and considerations of the above sort, are a poor substitute for what is really required in such cases —the extermination of pests which are destructive alike to field crops, to trees and shrubs, and to plants, and which offer at best a very scanty return for the havoc they commit.

LARGE-LEAFED ROCKFOIL in the Wild Garden.

CHAPTER XVI.

THE GARDEN OF BRITISH WILD FLOWERS AND TREES.

My learned and travelled friends who tell me I cannot naturalize Narcissus in thick grass, will hardly say we cannot grow our own lovely British tree willows, or have our own native Heaths in all their delightful variety growing near us in picturesque tangles, and some of our own more beautiful Wild Roses in the hedge! The passion for the exotic is so universal that our own finest plants are never planted, while money is thrown away like chaff for worthless exotic trees like the Wellingtonia, on which tree alone fortunes have been wasted. Once on the bank of a beautiful river in Ireland, the Barrow, I was shown a collection of ornamental Willows, and very interesting they were, but among them not one of our native Willows, which are not merely as good as any of the garden Willows but as good in beauty as the Olive tree—even where the Olive is most beautiful. We search the world over for flowering shrubs—not one of which is prettier than the Water Elder (Viburnum Opulus), common in Sussex woods, and often seen near the water-side in Surrey. Mr. Anthony Waterer, who has the finest nursery in England in our own day, told me that when asked for a number of it he could not find them in his own nursery, or in any other. As many of our beautiful wild flowers, and even our trees and shrubs, are strangers to our own gardens, I cannot do better than try to show, so far as I may, what beautiful things may be gathered from our British Flora that may have charms for our gardens and wild gardens. However well people may know the beauty of our fields and woods in spring or summer, few have any idea of the great number of flowers that are wild in our own country, and worth a home in gardens—at least in those of a picturesque nature. Few of us have much notion of the great variety of beauty that may be culled from British flowers alone. Many of us have full opportunity of seeing the beauties of the fields and hedges ; not so many the mountain plants, and few, such rare gems as Gentiana verna, which grows wild in Teesdale, and here and there on the western shores of Ireland ; or the mountain Forget-me-not, a precious little dwarf alpine that is found but rarely in the north. It is only by a good choice of the plants of the British Isles that we can hope to arrive at a ' garden of British plants.'

It is not only the curious and rare that may afford us interest among the plants of Britain ; among them are plants of much beauty. Even for the sake of plants for lakes, rivers, ponds in parks, pleasure grounds, or gardens, the subject is worthy attention. For the rock-garden, too, many of our wild flowers are fitted. In any part of the country where the soil or surface of the ground suits the habits of a variety of native plants, it would prove interesting to collect kinds not found in the neighbourhood, and naturalize them therein; and wherever the natural rock crops up, much beauty may be added by planting these rocky spots with wild mountain flowers.

'Botany,' says Emerson, 'is all names, not powers;' to press and dry wild plants is necessary for botanists, but it is not likely to cause any wide human interest in such things; and therefore I propose that we look through our British wild flowers with a view of giving some of them a home in the garden. It will be well to have a complete list of our wild flowers, which would be found in the index to Syme's, Bentham's, Babington's, or any other good book on our flora; but best is a list called the 'London Catalogue of British Plants,' which was published by Pamplin of Soho, and is now published by Bell in Covent Garden. This gives a full list of all the species, and by means of numbers indicates their distribution. The compilers adopted Mr. Hewett Watson's division of Britain into a number of botanical districts, and after the name of each species a number is placed, which tells the number of districts in which that particular plant is found.

Those who wish to work at wild flowers should get one of these lists, as on them may be at once marked the kinds we have or want; by their aid in part we may exchange the Orchids of the Surrey hills for the Alpines of the higher Scotch mountains, and so on throughout the country. Every admirer of British plants should have a manual, to aid in identifying the species. Another aid would be a 'local flora,' a list of the plants growing in any particular neighbourhood or county; such, for instance, as the 'Flora of Reigate,' Baine's 'Flora of Yorkshire,' and Mackay's 'Flora Hibernica,' or the 'Cybele Hibernica.' We will next turn to the plants, beginning with the natural order of Crowfoots. The Crowfoot order is the order which brightens the moist hollows in the spring with the glittering of the lesser Celandine, the meadows in May with Buttercups; when 'those long mosses in the stream' begin to assume a livelier green, 'and the wild Marsh Marigold shines like fire in swamps and hollows grey.' 'Those long mosses in the stream' of 'The Miller's Daughter' are the Water Crowfoots that silver over the pools with their pretty white cup-like blossoms in early summer; and it is the same family which burnishes our meadows with a glory of colour not equalled by any tropical flowers. But in considering British plants from a garden standpoint only, we can only seek those that are worthy of garden culture, and certain to reward us for giving them a place in the garden.

The first plant named in books of British Plants is the Traveller's Joy (Clematis Vitalba), the well-known common Clematis that streams over the trees, and falls in graceful folds from trees in many parts of the south of England, having in autumn heads of feathery awns. It is well known as a garden plant, and from its rapidity of growth nothing is better adapted for quickly covering rough mounds or bowers. However, it may be best used in the shrubbery, and particularly so on the margin of a river, or water, where the long streamers of its branchlets are graceful. It is the only native plant that gives an idea of the 'bush ropes' that run in wild profusion through tropical woods. We have the Meadow Rues, of one of which in this book is a figure as showing plants of some claim to beauty not often seen in the ordinary garden: the elegant lesser Meadow Rue (Thalictrum minus), so like the Maidenhair fern that some say it is as pretty for the open air as the Maidenhair fern is for the greenhouse. It is wild in many parts of Britain, in Scotland and north-western England, and rather abundant on the island of Ireland's Eye, near Dublin, and in many parts of the limestone districts of Clare and Galway. There are several other species, natives of Britain, but none of them showing any gain on this kind.

NATIVE WINDFLOWERS. Next come the Windflowers, or Anemones, four kinds, at least two of them — A. nemorosa, the wood Anemone, and A. apennina,

the blue Anemone — indispensable for our garden.
The wood Anemone is pretty either in its wild or
cultivated state, and besides the common white variety
there are a reddish and a double white variety.
The most beautiful form of our wood Anemone which
has come into the garden in our day is the large

ROBINSON'S BLUE WINDFLOWER.   A large sky-blue form of the wood Anemone.

sky-blue form.   I first saw it as a small tuft at
Oxford, and grew it in London where it was often
seen with me in bloom by Mr. Boswell Syme,
author of the Third Edition of Sowerby, who had
a great love for plants in a living state as well as
in their merely 'botanical' aspects, and we were

often struck with its singular charm about noon on bright days. There is reason to believe that there is both in England and Ireland a large and handsome form of the wood Anemone—distinct from the common white of our woods and shaws in spring, and that my blue Anemone is a variety of this. It is not the same as the blue form wild in parts of North Wales and elsewhere in Britain, this being more fragile looking and not so light a blue.

As for the Apennine blue Anemone it is one of the loveliest of spring flowers, both in the borders and scattered here and there in woods and shrubberies and grass. The flowers are freely produced, and of the loveliest blue. It is not a true but a naturalized native flower, so to speak, its home being the hills of South Europe, having escaped out of gardens into our land. The Pasque Anemone, or Pasque-flower, is a beautiful native plant bearing large flowers of a lovely violet purple, silky outside. It grows on limestone pastures, and occurs in several districts in England, though it is wanting in Scotland and Ireland. The Pasque-flower is one of those that are more beautiful in a wild than in a cultivated state, for though it grows freely in light and chalky soils in gardens, it has not half the beauty it shows in spring on the Downs. I never saw any plant more charming than this in the woods and hills and even on walls in Normandy in spring. Another kind, A. ranunculoides (yellow), is a doubtful native found in one or two spots, and pretty for chalky soils, on which it flowers freely. Being uncommon it is just the sort of plant to which those who have the right soil may give the hospitality of the garden.

Adonis autumnalis is the pretty 'pheasant's-eye,' an annual plant found in corn-fields, and of which the seed is offered in catalogues under the name of Flos Adonis.

The Ranunculi, or Crowfoots, begin with R. aquatilis and its several varieties, and several other species of Water Ranunculi with divided leaves. Few gardens offer any facilities for cultivating these. The most we can do is to introduce them to a pond or stream in which they are not already found, or add one of the long-leaved or rarer kinds to the common kind or kinds; but their home is in the fresh stream, 'hither, thither, idly playing,' or in the lake, and therefore they hardly come among garden plants. I have tried to grow all the kinds I could get, but the Canadian weed or the common R. aquatilis soon exterminated them. R. Ficaria is the pretty shining-leaved yellow kind, which abounds in moist and shaded places in spring; R. Flammula (the Spearwort) is a native of wet marshes and river-sides in all parts of Britain, and is well suited for planting by the water-side, though not so handsome as the greater Spearwort, R. Lingua, which is 2 or 3 feet high, and has large showy, yellow flowers. It is very fine near water, and is freely scattered over the British Isles, though not often plentiful. These plants must usually be collected in a wild state, though they are grown in some botanic gardens. R. acris pleno and R. repens pleno are double forms of the wild kinds, and worth growing, from their pretty ' bachelor's-button ' flowers, bright yellow, neat, double, lasting longer in flower than the single kinds.

Then we have the Marsh M arigold (Caltha palustris), which makes such a glorious show in spring along moist bottoms, or by river banks in rich soil—notably on the banks of the Thames, where, when in high tide, the ground for many feet under water looks as if strewn with gold, the water having overflowed numbers of these showy flowers. Even where common, in the woods and fields, this handsome plant, single or double, deserves a home beside all garden waters, or even in moist ground, because it makes a truly fine spring - flowering plant. There is a double variety sold in Covent Garden in early summer, bearing double flowers of large size, which, like the double Crowfoots, last longer than the single bloom. Apart from the double garden forms of the Marsh Marigold, these are the kinds now recognized as belonging to our flora.

Caltha.
palustris (Linn.).
    a. *vulgaris* (Schott).
    b. *Guerangerii* (Boreau).
    c. *minor* (Syme).
radicans (Forster).

Trollius europæus is the Globe-flower, well worthy of a garden home from its fine form, colour, and sweetness. Not a common plant in England, but frequent in the North and West, and in Ireland, it will grow in moist places and in clayey hollows often hopeless from weeds. I planted a large group in such a spot, and it has kept the weeds in check ever since, and gives us its welcome bloom every May. That pretty early spring flower, the Winter Aconite (Eranthis hyemalis), also belongs to this order, and is well worthy of culture. It is naturalized here and there, and is beautiful in light and chalky soils under trees in spring. The common Columbine (Aquilegia vulgaris) is often pretty. It is not common in the wild state, but a true native in several counties of England. In one gorge on Helvellyn I have seen it ascend almost to the top of that mountain, flowering beautifully in almost inaccessible spots; it is rather common in gardens, but in many and varied garden forms. The common poisonous Aconite (A. Napellus) is a fine native plant; it is, however, very common in gardens, where it should be kept quite isolated from any roots likely to be used as food, owing to its poisonous roots. Lastly, in the Buttercup order we have our native Helleborus (viridis and fœtidus), which will adorn rough banks with their evergreen leaves.

The common Berberis vulgaris, which is rather widely distributed, must not be forgotten, for there is no more beautiful sight afforded by any shrub than by this when draped over with its bright racemes of fruit. The white Water Lily, so common in our rivers, should be seen in all garden waters, not thickly planted, but a single specimen or group here and there. It is most effective when one or a few plants are seen alone on the water; then the flowers and leaves have full room to develop and float right regally; but when a dense crowd of water lilies are seen together, they crowd each other out. With it should be associated the yellow Water Lily (Nuphar lutea), and if it can be had, the smaller and rare Nuphar pumila.

Among the Poppies, the one best worth growing as a garden plant is the Welsh Poppy (Meconopsis Cambrica), which grows so abundantly along the road sides in the lake district. It is a perennial of a fine yellow, and thrives well at the bottom of walls and on stony banks. Some might care to grow the large Opium Poppy (P. somniferum); its finer double varieties are handsome, but these are scarcely British, the plant is naturalized. The field Poppy is everywhere in our corn-fields, and from it we get pretty races of Poppies, double and single. The Horned Poppy of our sea-shores is distinct and may be grown in a garden. Corydalis bulbosa is a dwarf early flower, scarcely a native, or rare; and the yellow fumitory (Corydalis lutea) is almost wonderful in its way of adorning walls and stony places, with the greatest differences as to soil and moisture.

In the natural order Cruciferæ, Thlaspi alpestre (a pretty Alpine), Iberis amara (a fine white annual), Draba aizoides (a rare and beautiful Alpine), Koniga maritima, the sweet Alyssum, and Dentaria bulbifera, rare, and curious ; the Ladies' Smock, and its double variety; Arabis petræa, a sweet dwarf alpine ; the common Wallflower, and the Single Rocket (Hesperis matronalis) and the Sea-kale of our shores are worth growing.

All the British Helian-themum or Sun Roses, and the annual kind H. guttatum of the Channel Islands, are pretty plants. Many do not know we have a list so full as this of native kinds :—

Helianthemum.
guttatum (Mill).
Breweri (Planch.).
marifolium (Mill).
  b. *vineale* (Pers.).
Chamæcistus (Mill).
polifolium (Mill).

Native Sun Rose in Somerset Combe.

These of course apart from the garden forms of the common sun rose which are numerous. Of the violets, in addition to the sweet violet, which should be grown on a north aspect, V. lutea and V. tricolor will be found the most distinct and worthy of culture. Apart from the many garden varieties there are the white and various wild forms. The interesting little Milkworts, which are so pretty on our sandy and chalky hills, are very rarely grown—though they well might be in a garden of native rock or heath and down plants. The very dwarf trailing Frankenia lævis (Sea Heath) runs over stones, and looks neat and mossy on a rock-garden. In the Pink tribe, the scarce, single, wild Carnation (D. Caryophyllus), D. plumarius, the parent of the garden pink, and the Cheddar Pink, which thrives on an old wall, D. deltoides, the maiden pink, the soapwort (Saponaria officinalis), the Sea-bladder Campion (Silene maritima), Silene acaulis, the beautiful little Alpine that clothes our higher mountains, the Corn Cockle (Lychnis Githago), the Ragged Robin, and the Alpine Lychnis; the vernal sandwort (Arenaria verna), Arenaria ciliata, found on Ben Bulben, in Ireland, and Cerastium alpinum are among the prettiest. The last is as shaggy as a Skye terrier, and does not grow more than an inch high.

A pretty species of Flax is not a common plant in British gardens, but one occurs wild in some of our eastern counties,—Linum perenne,—a blue-flowered plant, of which there is a pure white variety, both very pretty plants, quite hardy and perennial. The perennial Flax, or any of its varieties, will be found to thrive in any place where the grass is not mown as well as on borders. The field flax is sometimes found wild with us, but it is not a true native. Among the Malva tribe we have several showy plants, but less worthy of garden cultivation, except it be Lavatera arborea (the tree Lavatera), sparsely found along the south and west coasts. It is a plant of fine habit, growing 5 or 6 feet high. The best of the Mallows is the Musk Mallow (M. moschata), which has showy flowers, and is a charming native flower by streams and on banks: it is a very good garden plant, especially the white form.

The St. John's Worts (Hypericum) have some beauty, and might find a place among low shrubs; the best perhaps is H. calycinum, or 'St. John's Wort,' a kind which is not perhaps truly British, but which is now naturalized in parts of England and Ireland. The showy flowers of this and its habit fit it for the garden; and it is particularly adapted for rough banks, or will crawl freely under and near trees, though it will best show its beauty when fully exposed to the sun and air. It should not be used as a 'carpet' under old or favourite trees, as it will sometimes starve and kill trees.

In the Geranium order there are a few pretty plants for the garden—notably, G. pratense, G. sylvaticum, and G. sanguineum, with its fine variety G. lancastriense. This variety was originally found in the Isle of Walney, in Lancashire, and some writers have made it a species under the name of G. lancastriense. Both plants are well worth growing in a garden. G. sanguineum makes a very pretty border plant, or for forming groups between shrubs. The stubwort (Oxalis Acetosella) is the prettiest among its British allies; and a chaste little plant it is, too, when seen in shady, woody places, along hedge-banks, and over mossy stumps; in gardens where there is a little diversity of surface, or half shady spots, it might be grown with advantage where it does not come of itself. Some say it is the Shamrock of the ancient Irish, but they are wrong. Custom among the Irish, during the experience of the oldest people, and everything that can be gleaned, point to the common Trifolium repens as the true Shamrock.

In the Pea order there are a few plants of great merit, and the first we meet with is the very pretty dwarf shrub Genista tinctoria, or Dyer's genista. This is a little shrub, but vigorous in the profusion of its yellow flowers, and would be at home on any rough banks or grassy places, or among dwarf shrubs. It is frequent in England, but rare in Scotland and Ireland. Its two allies, G. pilosa and G. anglica, are also neat little shrubs, both worth a place among dwarf British shrubs.

Many who care for wild flowers must have been struck with the beauty of the common Restharrow, which spreads such delicate colour over many a chalk cliff and sandy pasture. It bears garden culture well, and is prettier when in flower than numbers of New Holland plants, which require protection. There is a smoother and more bushy form of this sometimes admitted as a species, Ononis antiquorum, which is also a fine plant, growing freely from seed, and of the easiest culture.

The Bird's-foot trefoil, though common, is so beautiful that it must not be forgotten, flowering as it does nearly the whole summer. There are several forms of it and few better plants for the front edge of borders. The Lady's Fingers (Anthyllis vulneraria) is a pretty plant found in chalky pastures and dry stony places in England.

The three native kinds of Astragalus are worthy of cultivation, and so are the allied plants, Oxytropis. Both O. campestris and O. uralensis are dwarf plants, the foliage of the last being silvery. The first is found only in one spot among the Clova mountains in Scotland ; the second is rather common on the Scotch hills. Hippocrepis comosa is rather like the Bird's-foot trefoil, both in habit and flower, and is worth a place among rock plants.

Of the Vetches two at least are worthy of culture— V. Cracca and V. sylvatica. The first makes a charming border plant if slightly supported on stakes, so that it may have hidden its supports by the time the flowers appear. The wood Vetch is of a climbing habit, and very elegant when seen running up the stems of young trees or over bushes. This is found in most woody hills of Britain and Scotland, and V. Cracca is common everywhere.

Among native peas the best is the Sea Pea (Lathyrus maritimus), a handsome plant in rich ground. It occurs on the coast of southern and eastern England, of Shetland, and of Kerry, in Ireland.

In the Rose order both the Spiræas should interest us—certainly S. Filipendula, which has leaves cut somewhat like a fern. The double variety is pretty. Dryas octopetala, a plant found on the limestone mountains of North England and Ireland, and abundantly in Scotland, is a pretty little rock evergreen bush.

NATIVE BRIERS AND WILD ROSES.

As for the blackberry, raspberry, dewberry, and cloudberry, some may desire to cultivate them, and it is very interesting to observe the differences between some of the sub-species and varieties of blackberries, and the beauty, both in fruit and flower, of the family. Many people, even among those who care for trees and shrubs, have little idea of the variety existing among our native Brambles. Over ninety species and their varieties and wild forms are given in the last edition of the 'London Catalogue'! The question of whether these are true species or merely varieties need not trouble us, for plants showing very slight distinction to a botanist may be essentially distinct in beauty and effect. A man might do a more foolish thing than get these together and grow them on some rough bank or corner or even in newly-made banks of hedgerows There is much beauty of leaf among the plants, and variety in the quality of the fruit, some of the kinds being valuable for their fruit. Whatever we may do with brambles, however, our native wild roses deserve a place in fence or hedgerow, or rough banks if convenient. Some indeed come of themselves, but it would be very interesting to grow many of the less common kinds and consider them for their beauty. Botanic gardens might well show us such fine families as these, instead of rivalling the pastry-cook 'bedding' of the private gardener, and I do not remember ever seeing any attempt to grow them except in the Cambridge Botanic Garden, the curator of which writes as follows of our wild roses.

'We all allow the Roses of the florist to be without rival among flowers of the garden, and we can but admit that wild Roses are perhaps the most lovely flowers of the field. But there are numbers of the wildings, and all beautiful, and some of surpassing charm. We want to see them more often grown in our gardens. Sometimes we admire a chance seedling, as, for instance, in the Cambridge Botanic Garden, where some years ago R. dumalis (a form of the Dog Rose) took possession of a Spruce Fir, and now attains to a height of about twenty feet, forming wreaths of blossom in summer. The Spruce is dead, but the Rose still clings to the old stem, which forms just the right kind of support. Such an object as this, or Rosa arvensis, in the collection, makes us wonder why these single Roses have not received more attention. They are usually so robust, just what is wanted for pleasure grounds and the wild garden, and then in autumn we frequently have their brilliant red fruit. At this moment in some of the hedges of the neighbourhood are shrubs with quantities of fruit, which in a garden would help considerably in colour effect.

'To show what material there is, I may mention that the many forms of our native roses fall under seven distinct aggregate groups.

'We have first the well-known Scotch or Burnet Rose (R. spinosissima), lovely with white or pink flowers; next,

THE FIELD ROSE (R. arvensis). Engraved from a picture in the possession of Mrs. L. Maxse.

R. villosa, which in various forms makes a large bush, with erect or arching branches, very hairy leaves and densely glandular sepals. It is distinguished from the last-mentioned by its larger size and equal prickles, and from R. canina by its straight prickles. Under it we have R. tomentosa, with a large pale pink flower, and R. mollissima, with a smaller, deeper-coloured flower. The succeeding species is R. involuta, under which are numerous kinds, small and erect, with short branches and crowded prickles, passing into bristles. Among them we may note R. Wilsoni, with bright red flowers, and R. Sabini, with ample foliage and pale pink flowers. Next is our fragrant R. rubiginosa, the sweet Brier, which, however, is less fragrant, as it approaches R. canina and R. villosa. Near to this species we may mention R. macrantha and R. sepium, both of which have rather pretty flowers, though they are somewhat small. R. hibernica is the next species to refer to, and it is intermediate between R. spinosissima and R. canina, though most like the latter. It is small and erect, with short, sometimes arching branches and erect globose naked fruit. It is figured with pale pink flowers. Rosa canina is the familiar Dog Rose, of which the varieties are very numerous. It has long arching branches, with stout hooked prickles, having a thickened base, and in the common form is the strongest-growing of British Roses. It is often very beautiful, and, all things considered, some of the best results may no doubt be got from this species. R. cæsia and R. incana, belonging to this species, have glaucous leaves. The foliage of R. Bakeri is very pretty, and R. dumalis is a fine tall kind, but the varieties of this species are so numerous, that it is difficult to specify. Our last species is R. arvensis, known from R. canina by the union of the styles into a long slender column, that species having the styles free. There

are two sub-species, R. arvensis proper (R. repens) having
the leaflets glabrous, glaucous beneath, and R. stylosa with
leaflets pubescent beneath. This last connects R. arvensis
with R. canina, and under it the several varieties occur.
The variety Monsoniæ, found in a hedge at Watford, has
very large red flowers and sub-globose, orange-red fruit. It
is our present R. arvensis proper to which the Ayrshire Rose
must be referred. The flowers are more cup-shaped than
those of any other British Rose, and Lindley says that
Sabine had a variety with pink flowers. No illustration has
before appeared in any journal, but a figure in " English
Botany " shows to some extent what a fine thing it is. The
plant has long, trailing shoots, with small, scattered prickles,
oval leaflets, glabrous on both surfaces, and glaucous or
whitish green beneath. The flowers are of elegant outline,
with pure white corolla, except the throat, which is yellow,
and have a purple calyx; and the fruit is scarlet when ripe.

Sloe, Bullace, Wild Cherry, Rowan, Wild Service, White Beam, Wild Pear, Crab, Medlar, May.

These are native trees—some of them of much
beauty, taking great share in the landscape beauty of
our country, and a place in its literature—some of
them also being the source of our best hardy fruits.
I wish to plead for their use in the wild garden, if
not in the garden itself. What is more beautiful in
the landscape than a snowy wreath of old sloe trees
in spring, seen beyond the wide fields, or more

delicate in bud when seen at hand? The Wild Cherry, Rowan, White Beam, and Crab do their own part in adorning our woods, but we need not leave them wholly there. I find the Medlar charming for its leaves in the fall as well as for the large simple flowers in spring, and make groups of it on the grass. The May is the one loved tree that all enjoy: there are several wild forms in Britain besides the garden varieties:—

Cratægus.
Oxyacantha (Linn.).
  a. *oxyacanthoides* (Thu.).
  b. *laciniata* (Wallr.).
  c. *kyrtostyla* (Fingerh.).
  d. *monogyna* (Jacq.).

To remind the reader of how much tree beauty there is in this now obscure corner of our flora—so far as gardens go—I print here the names of the wild kinds of these trees so far as known to us now, with their English names where they have any.

Prunus.
communis (Huds.)—Sloe.
  b. *fruticans* (Weihe).
insititia (Linn.)—Bullace.
Avium (Linn.)—Gean.
Cerasus (Linn.)—Wild Cherry.
Padus (Linn.)—Bird Cherry.

Pyrus.
torminalis (Ehrh.)—Wild service.
Aria (Sm.)—White Beam.
  b. *rupicola* (Syme).
latifolia (Syme).

Pyrus (*continued*).
   scandica (Syme).
   hybrida (Linn.).
   Aucuparia (Gaert.) — Rowan.
   communis (Linn.) – Pear.
     a. *Pyraster* (Linn.).
     b. *Achras* (Gært.).
     c. *cordata* (Desv.).
   Malus (Linn.)—Apple.
     a. *acerba* (DC.).
     b. *mitis* (Wallr.).
   Germanica (Linn.)—Medlar.

The Cloudberry can be grown best in a wet, boggy soil, and is difficult of culture as a garden plant, except in moist and elevated spots. The dewberry, distinguished principally by the glaucous bloom on the fruit when ripe, is of easy culture. Of the Potentillas, P. rupestris, white-flowered, found on the Breiddin Hills in Montgomeryshire, and the large yellow P. alpestris, from the higher limestone mountains, are the best. P. fruticosa, of the north of England, and in Clare and Galway, in Ireland, is a free flowering low bush; and the marsh potentilla (P. Comarum) will do well in boggy ground, if we have it, though it is more distinct than pretty.

The common willow-herb (Epilobium angustifolium), so showy, and so apt to become a bad weed, is well known. But, in a wood or out-of-the-way spot, where it cannot overrun rarer plants, it is very pretty. Even the botanist, in describing it, says, 'a handsome plant'—an expression very seldom used by gentlemen who write on English botany.

The Evening Primrose (Œnothera biennis) deserves a place from its fragrance; and it is as well to sow it in some out-of-the-way spot. It often covers waste building ground in London.

Next we have the Loosestrife (Lythrum Salicaria), a water-side plant, abundant in many parts of Britain. There is a variety of this plant known in gardens by the name of L. roseum superbum, which should be in and by every pond. The Common Herniary (Herniaria glabra) and Scleranthus perennis are two very dwarf green spreading plants, found in some of the southern and central counties of England, and which give a neat Lycopodium-like effect in the rock-garden.

Then we come to the Rose-root (Sedum Rhodiola) and the tribe of pretty Stonecrops (Sedum), every one of which is worthy of a place on the rock-garden—from the common stonecrop, which grows on the thatch of cottages and abundantly in many parts of Britain, on rocky places, to that little gem for a wall, Sedum dasy-phyllum of the south of England. The Rose-root is so called from the drying root-stock smelling like roses. The Orpine or Livelong (Sedum Telephium) is also a fine old plant of this order. If you have any old walls or buildings, try and establish a few of the smaller kinds on these; it is interesting to have rare plants established in such places, and the tenderer kinds will always survive on walls, whereas they may get cut off by the winter on the ground. Fern-growers find it difficult to establish the little Wall Rue (Asplenium Ruta-muraria) in pots, pans, or any way in the fernery ; but by taking a few of the spore-bearing fronds, and shaking a little of the ' fern-seed ' into the chinks of an old wall, we may soon establish it ; and in like manner it is quite possible to cultivate the Ceterach and the graceful Spleenwort, only that the wall must be somewhat older, so to speak, to accommodate these than the Wall Rue, as this little fern will grow on a wall that is in perfect condition, as may be seen at Lord Mansfield's at Highgate, where the high garden-wall that runs for some distance parallel with the road running from Hampstead to Highgate is covered in its upper part with this plant. In gardening few things are more interesting than an old wall covered with ferns and rock and mountain plants.

The Stonecrops are followed in the natural classification of British plants by the Rockfoils (Saxifraga), like the Stonecrops in size, but more valuable for the garden. First, there is the Irish group of Saxifrages, the London Pride and its varieties ; and the Killarney Saxifrage, S. Geum and its interesting varieties, both species very pretty for the rock-garden and borders. Next we have the mountain S. stellaris and S. nivalis, and the yellow marsh S. Hirculus, and the yellow S. Aizoides, which fringes the rills and streams on the hills and mountains in Scotland, and the north of England and Ireland, all interesting, but surpassed in beauty by the purple Saxifraga oppositifolia, which opens its bright flowers soon after the snow melts in the Scotch Highlands, and as far north, among the higher mountains of Europe and Asia, as the Arctic Circle. It bears garden culture well, on the rock-garden, or in patches in the front of a border, planted in the full sun.

The meadow (Saxifraga granulata) differs in most respects from most of the other Rockfoils, and is worth growing; its double variety, seen in cottage gardens, is used for the spring garden. It flowers so well that the very leaves are hidden by large double flowers. It is frequently found in small cottage gardens in Surrey.

The dense green mossy Rockfoils are precious for the garden, from the living green which they take on in winter, when all else fades—when the fallen leaves rush by, driven by the winds of autumn—and when geraniums and all the fleeting flower-garden things are cut off. These mossy Rockfoils grow on almost any soil or situation, and may be grown with ease even in towns. They are dotted over with white flowers in early summer, the stems of which should be cut off as soon as the flowers perish, but their greatest charm is in winter. S. hypnoides, abundant in Scotland, Wales, and northern England, with its varieties, is our best plant in this way; and S. cæspitosa, found on some of the higher Scotch mountains, is allied to it, and also good. In towns shrubs do not keep their verdure, through various adverse influences; in all places these mossy Rockfoils charm us with their verdure if we take the trouble to put them in bold flakes on the rock-garden or on borders, or to use them as a carpet beneath tea and other roses. There are many forms of the mossy Rockfoil, natives of Britain.

Next we have the beautiful Grass of Parnassus (Parnassia palustris), a distinct and charming native plant, rather frequent in Britain in bogs and moist heaths. I have grown it very successfully in a small artificial bog, and still better in 6-inch pots in peat soil, the pots being placed in a saucer of water during summer, and preserved in a cold frame in winter. It is, however, much better to 'naturalize' it in moist grassy places than to grow it in this way.

The Spignel or Baldmoney (Meum athamanticum), of the Scotch highlands, Wales, and the north of England, having elegantly divided leaves, and being very neat in habit, is an interesting border or rock plant. Among the plants of the umbelliferous order there are not many native plants worthy of cultivation, except the Sea-Holly (Eryngium maritimum), and the sweet Cicely (Myrrhis odorata), often cultivated in old times and gardens for various uses; not a rare plant, but most plentiful in the hilly parts of the north of England. This for its odour and foliage is welcome in the garden, and groups of it are pretty between shrubs. The sweet Fennel, which is often seen wild in the south on chalk banks, is a graceful plant, and typical of the great beauty of form, which belongs to many plants of the order. For the rest of this numerous order they are best seen in a wild state where their effects are often striking—particularly in some rich woods. The Twin-flower (Linnæa borealis) is one of the most charming among our native plants, trailing as it does so prettily in fir woods in the north. It is found, though rarely, in Scotland ; and it may be grown easily in gardens in moist peat, or cool sandy parts of the rock-garden or cool borders, and may indeed be naturalized in peaty soil with a sparse growth.

Natural growth of umbellate plants.

Of our native Dogwoods (Cornus), one (sanguinea) is an excellent native shrub, the beauty of which is very effective in gardens where it is grouped in bold and artistic ways. The winter effect is bright and good, and the plant fine for association with our handsomer native willows : this Dogwood being used as undergrowth

near the largest willows. The little native Cornel is
a charming alpine and bog plant. Our native woodbine
appeals to all, so I need hardly tell of its beauty : the
value of our native Viburnums is not so well known—
few shrubs of any countries are so handsome in blossom
and berry as the Water Elder (V. Opulus)—so called in
some of the home counties, from its frequence on river
banks, though common too in underwoods. The other
is the wayfaring tree (V. Lantana) common in hedgerows in the south, its berries conspicuous in autumn.

OUR NATIVE HEATHS. Of the variety and beauty of
our native heaths few have much idea. The wild
species are beautiful ; from time to time varieties have
appeared amongst them which nurserymen have preserved ; and in a collection of these, the variety of gay
colour is charming. I had no idea of the beauty of
colour afforded by the varieties till I visited the Comely
Bank nurseries at Edinburgh a few years ago, and there
found a large area of ground covered with their exquisite
colours, and looking like a beautiful flower garden. But
if all this beauty did not exist, the charms of the common
species, as spread out even on our southern heaths,
should lead us to give the heaths a good place in the
picturesque garden.

All species and varieties are worthy of a place, beginning with the varieties of the common Ling (Calluna
vulgaris)—the commonest of all heaths. It has 'sported'
into a great number of varieties, many of which are
preserved in nurseries. Some of them are bright and

distinct in colour ; others differ distinctly in habit, some close to the ground in dense bushes. There is no more beautiful shrub than the native Heather in its commonest form, so that it is easy to judge of the value of the fine white and other forms if we use them well : as to vigour, the plant may be often seen flourishing on banks with little soil on them, and the same fine vigour is true of the varieties—excluding merely monstrous and variegated forms. Then we have the ' Scotch heather ' (Erica cinerea), the reddish purple showy flowers of which are very attractive, but surpassed in beauty of colour by a variety of the same plant, coccinea ; and there is also a white variety, as there is of the Bell Heather (Erica tetralix), to which is also closely related the Irish E. Mackaiana. Next we have the ciliated Heath (E. ciliaris), a pretty kind, with flowers nearly as large as those of St. Daboec's heath, and the Irish heath (E. hibernica), found in some of the western counties of Ireland. Finally, we have among these interesting plants the Cornish Heath (E. vagans), and from what has been said of the family it will be seen what interesting beds or groups might be made from these alone, grown almost anywhere. Our object should be to make the most of natural advantages, and as many persons must have gardens suited for what are called American plants, they would find it worth while to devote a spot to our Heaths and their varieties. It is charming to form a garden of bold beds of these, as the late Sir W. Bowman did so well in Surrey, but the most

artistic way is to form bold masses of these Heaths
without the garden proper, on rough banks and the
outer parts of the grounds. It is an error to suppose that peat is required for these plants. Even in
1893—the year of many sunny months and days—
I often saw the Heather in bloom on stony railway
banks in Sussex, often facing the sun; and that
same year too when staying at Coolhurst I saw the
prettiest possible foreground to a house in the home
counties at Newells—a field of Heather in full bloom
with the rich weald seen across it. This field had,
I think, come of itself. Where we seek to establish
the heaths in the way named above it is best to get
them in some quantity from growers who offer them
in liberal numbers: to set my picturesque beds I
plant in large masses in well-dug ground, but once
established leave the beds alone, and allow them to
grow together in their own way. I must state here
for those who will not take the trouble to understand,
that these Heath beds are *not* in my flower garden.

Nearly allied to the Heaths we have the interesting
bog Vaccinium, which may be cultivated in marshy
or peaty ground. To these belong the cranberry,
bilberry, and whortleberry; and for some of these
and the American kinds, people have ere now made
artificial bogs in their gardens. The little creeping
evergreen, Arctostaphylos uva-ursi, or bearberry, is
neat in the rock-garden. It is found in hilly districts
in Scotland, northern England, and Ireland. Then

the Marsh Andromeda (A. polifolia), found chiefly in central and northern England, bears very pretty pink flowers, and grows freely in peat. The very small English Azalea (procumbens) is also a very interesting native plant, forming a cushiony bush not more than a couple of inches high. In Britain it is found only in the Scotch highlands. I have only once seen this well established in a garden. Few people who admire what are called peat shrubs can have failed to notice from time to time the beautiful St. Daboec's Heath (Menziesia polifolia), a plant found abundantly on the heathy wastes of the Asturias and in south-western France, and also in Connemara, in Ireland. It is usually associated with 'American plants' in our nurseries and gardens, liking peat soil, and is a beautiful plant. The flowers are usually pink, and there is a white variety even more beautiful. The very rare blue Menziesia of the Sow of Athol, in Perthshire, is also charming. The Pyrolas, or Winter-greens, are very pretty native plants, some of them fragrant. P. rotundifolia and P. uniflora are among the best, and both are rare, flourishing in moist sandy soils, as they do between the sand-hills on the coast of Lancashire. The periwinkles, Vinca minor and V. major, and their forms, are well known, and they often garland banks and hedgerow bottoms.

One of the most precious gems in the British flora is the vernal Gentian (G. verna), which grows in Teesdale and on the western shores of Ireland. The blue of this flower is most vivid; it is one of the most charming of all Alpine flowers, and should be in every garden ‚of hardy plants, on the rock-garden, or borders where only dwarf plants are grown. It may be grown well in sandy loam mixed with broken limestone or gravel, and indeed is not particular as to soil, provided that it be mixed with sharp sand or grit, and kept moist, and left for several years undisturbed. It is best suited for a level spot on

THE VERNAL GENTIAN. (Engraved from a photograph.)

the rock-garden with a good body of soil into which its roots may descend. It may be grown in rock-gardens, the surface of the ground being studded here and there with small stones, among which this lovely plant will grow and flower. It is abundant in mountain pastures in central and southern Europe; it is, in fact, a true Alpine, and may now be had in various nurseries.

It cannot be too well known that 'rock-works,' as generally made, are ugly, unnatural, and quite unfit for a plant to grow upon. The stones or 'rocks' are piled up, with no sufficient quantity of soil or any preparation made for the plants, so that all delicate rock-plants die upon them, and the 'rocks' are taken possession of by rank weeds. These rock-gardens are generally made too perpendicular, even in the best gardens in England—masses of rock being used merely to produce an effect, or masses of stone piled up without any of those chinks of soil into which rock-plants delight to root. The best way is to have more soil than 'rock,' to let the latter suggest itself rather than expose its uncovered sides, and to make them very much flatter than is the rule, so that the moisture may freely enter in every direction, and that the rock-garden may more resemble a cropping out of stone or rocks than the ridiculous wall-like structures which pass for rock-gardens.

The Marsh Gentian (G. Pneumonanthe) is also a lovely plant, which should have a moist spot in a border, and is not difficult to find in the north of England; also, less plentifully, in central and southern England. The Brighton Horticultural Society is in the habit of giving prizes for collections of wild plants, and thereby doing much harm by causing a few rude collectors to gather bunches of the rarest wild flowers, and perhaps exterminate them. When at one of its meetings a few years ago, I observed among the collections competing for a trifling prize large bunches of this beautiful Gentian, which had been pulled up by the roots, to form one of one hundred or more bunches of wild flowers torn up by one individual. In the Gentian order we have also the beautiful Bogbean (Menyanthes trifoliata), a plant that will grow on the margin of water or ditches or ponds ; it will also grow and flower in a moist border. It is a well-known plant almost everywhere in Britain ; a beautiful native flower elegantly fringed on the inside with white filaments, and its unopened buds tipped with apple-blossom red. Villarsia nymphæoides is also another pretty water-plant, with floating, small, water-lily-like leaves, and, in July, many yellow flowers—so many as to give a very showy effect ; and it associates well with the white water-lily. One of the prettiest effects I have ever seen was produced by this plant lining a small bay with a group of water-lilies on its outer side. Seen from the opposite shore the effect was charming—large water-lilies in front, then a wide-spreading mass of green sprinkled with starry yellow, and behind the shrubs which came to the water's edge on the shores of the little bay.

Jacob's Ladder, or Greek Valerian as it is sometimes called, also belongs to the Gentian order, and is a border plant, and its variegated variety (Polemonium cæruleum variegatum) is much used in fine flower gardens.

Most worthy of notice, in the Galium tribe, is the little white-starred Woodruff (Asperula odorata), which grows profusely in many British woods in spring. Where not wild, it should be grown in gardens, even if only for its fragrance. It is as sweet as the new hay, and continues to give forth its odour for a long time. When green, the 'haulm' of this plant betrays no very noticeable fragrance, but begins to emit it very soon after being cut, and merely requires to be placed on some dry shelf or half-open drawer, where it may get quite dry.

The common Red Valerian, as it is called, or Centranthus ruber botanically, is a handsome plant, on banks, borders, or rocky places and walls. As it may be readily raised from seed, there can be no difficulty in procuring it, and it should be noted that there is a fine deep red as well as the ordinary variety, and also a pure white one. Like the Wall-flower, they do well on old walls and bridges, and thus have become 'naturalized' in many parts of the country. It is the first plant that comes up in newly-opened chalk-pits.

The Hieraciums are often beautiful plants, as may be well seen in Mr. Hanbury's book now in progress. Many of them may be grown on rock-gardens or on well-exposed borders of dwarf plants. Such plants as these, the beauty of which is so little known in gardens, should be taken up by persons who like to get out of formal tracks, as botanical books rarely or never show the beauty of plants as they grow, and as very few have opportunities of seeing the plants on the hills when in flower. One who grew the more beautiful species might give rare pleasure to people who cared for our native mountain plants.

Silybum Marianum, the Milk thistle; Carduus erio-phorus, a noble thistle—found chiefly in the limestone districts of the south of England—and the great, woolly, silvery Cotton thistle, as it is often called, are hand-some plants. One isolated plant or a group or two will be sufficient for ordinary gardens; but where there is sufficient space these, with many other fine wild plants, might be naturalized by sowing a few of the seeds in any waste place, or in the shrubbery. The Milk thistle, with its shining green leaves and white markings, is very desirable among the British plants, though scarcely so much so as the great Cotton thistle.

The common Corn-flower (Centaurea Cyanus) is a beautiful garden plant, if sown in autumn: sown in spring, it is not so strong. I know of nothing more beautiful than a bold group of the Corn-flower in spring and early summer; the bloom is so lasting, the flowers so pretty for cutting. One of the prettiest of dwarf trailing silvery plants is the woolly Diotis maritima, which is found on the southern shores of England, coming up as far as Anglesea on the west and Suffolk on the east, but generally a rare plant in this country. The double variety of the Pyrethrum, now so frequent in our flower gardens, is a native plant—or, at least, the single or normal form of the species is. The Sea Wormwood (Artemisia maritima) forms a silvery bush, common on our shores, and worthy a corner now and then in our gardens. There is a deep rose-coloured variety of the common Yarrow, which should be in every garden, and there is a very pretty double white variety of the 'Sneezewort' (Achillea Ptarmica) which comes from British parents.

The Mountain Everlasting (Gnaphalium dioicum) is a beautiful dwarf plant, admirable for rocks or the front of a border, or in any way amongst Alpine plants; it abounds on mountains in Scotland, Wales, and many parts of England. There is a variety called G. d. roseum, that has its dwarf flowers delicately tinted with rose; neat edgings are sometimes made of this plant, so that there should be no difficulty in procuring it, even supposing we cannot find it wild; it is a popular plant wherever Alpine flowers are grown.

We will now turn to the extensive Harebell order, where we shall find much beauty, from the Harebell which swings its pretty blue above the wind-beaten turf on many an upland pasture, to the little prostrate Ivy Campanula (C. hederacea), plentiful in moist spots in Ireland and western England.

The giant Campanula (C. latifolia) is one of the handsomest, and is pretty frequent. The Spreading Campanula (C. patula), of the central and southern counties of England, is also very ornamental. C. Trachelium is also good, and indeed nearly all the plants of the family are pretty; but none of them surpass in beauty the common Harebell, which, although it may struggle for existence on poor or exposed pastures, yet, when transferred to a garden, makes a vigorous plant and flowers profusely—a mass of pleasing colour.

The little Ivy Campanula had better be grown in a pan of peat soil, or in some moist and slightly shaded spot where it may not be overrun by tall plants. Both this plant and the even more interesting Linnæa borealis may be grown well on the outside of the window, with a north or shady aspect, during the seven warmest months of the year, by planting them in pots of peat earth, and standing these in pans of water.

The Ivy-leaved Cyclamen, or the common Cyclamen (Cyclamen hederæfolium), a native of Southern Europe, but not supposed to be truly British, has been found in several places, apparently wild, and as such is generally included among British plants. Being a beautiful plant, it is worthy of a place. We cannot easily find it wild in England, but it is not difficult to obtain, and a lovely plant it is when seen in flower. A ring of it planted round a small bed of choice shrubs forms a pretty sight, and it may be naturalized, in bare places, in woods and shrubberies. The Water Violet (Hottonia palustris) with its whorls of pale purple flowers is a pretty plant for ponds or ditches.

I had almost forgotten our native Primroses and

Cowslips, but there is no need to plead for these and
their numerous and beautiful varieties. The Bird's
Eye Primrose of northern England—one of the sweetest
of our native plants—is, however, very rarely seen in
gardens. It would thrive well in wet spots on pastures
and heaths, and also in bare moist spots by the side of
rivulets, and in the bog bed, as would the smaller and
beautiful Scotch Bird's Eye Primrose.

The Loosestrifes, or Lysimachias, are pretty for
cultivation; L. Nummularia, the Creeping Jenny of the
London windows, trailing its luxuriant leaves where few
other plants would thrive so well. The upright-growing
species L. thyrsiflora is good for the margin of water,
in consequence of the curious habit it has of half-
hiding its flowers among the green of its leaves;
a mass of it by a river, or pond, or ditch, looks very
distinct and pleasing. Finally, we have in the Primula
order the beautiful Trientalis of the north, a wood
plant, and somewhat difficult to cultivate, but one that
may be grown in shady and half-shady spots in peat soil.

Of the Thrift family, certainly the most valuable
plant is a deep and charming rose-coloured variety of
the common Thrift (Armeria vulgaris). Everybody
knows the Thrift of our sea-shores, and of the tops of
some of the Scotch Mountains, with its pale pink
flowers; but the variety named here is of a showy rose,
and one of the plants we can use in the spring garden
as an edging plant, or in borders. This kind is sold
and known as Armeria vulgaris rubra. Any of the

British Statices that may be collected are worthy
a place in a collection of wild flowers.

Euphorbia Lathyris is the stately Caper Spurge,
which is established here and there with us; it is
worthy of a place, though not for the beauty of its
flowers. Nor must we forget the common Hop
(Humulus lupulus) which is graceful when well grown
over a bower.

The beautiful 'Poet's Narcissus' (Narcissus poeticus),
hawked about the streets of London so abundantly in
spring, is generally included in native plants, though
not considered truly British; but whether it be so or
not, such a distinctly beautiful plant should be in every
garden. The Snowflake (Leucojum æstivum) occurs
in several of the south-eastern counties, and makes
a handsome border plant; the dwarf, sweet, and fine
vernal Snowflake has been recently found in Dorset-
shire in some abundance; while the common Snowdrop
is freely naturalized in various parts of the country.
These, it need hardly be said, should all be in any
collection of British wild flowers, and with them the
Daffodil and the Wood-tulip (Tulipa sylvestris). This
last is found most frequently in some of the eastern
counties of England, but may be had readily from the
nurserymen, who sell it as T. florentina and cornuta.
Lloydia serotina is an extremely rare little bulbous
plant, found in North Wales. It is also known as
Anthericum serotinum.

Among native bulbs there are some very interesting.

The Snake's Head (Fritillaria meleagris) is abundant in some parts of the south and east of England, and it is worthy of a place in a garden. I know of nothing prettier in the spring garden than the singular suspended bells of the English Fritillary, often so prettily spotted, and occasionally white. The white form is a plant to encourage in every garden, the large white

SNOWFLAKE (Longleat).

bells being so distinct. The two British Scilla, though not so pretty as some of the continental species, so conspicuous among spring flowers, must not be forgotten in a full collection, nor the varieties of the wood hyacinth, and there are several of interest, both white and pink. The Two-leaved Lily of the Valley (Convallaria bifolia) is a diminutive and sweet little herb, found in only a few localities, and thriving on rocky borders and banks among dwarf plants. It is common on the Continent, and may be readily had from some nurseries, and in all botanic gardens in this country.

The common Lily of the Valley is a true native plant, abundant in some counties, though wanting in others. The graceful Solomon's Seal (Polygonatum multiflorum) and the Lily of the Valley should be planted to establish themselves in a semi-wild state in every place which has a shrubbery or wood. The Star of Bethlehem (Ornithogalum umbellatum) and the drooping O. nutans are established in several parts of the country. The first is a well-known old garden plant; the second a handsome kind with drooping flowers. To these we may add the Meadow Saffron (Colchicum autumnale), abundant in parts of Ireland and England, and frequently cultivated as a garden plant, commonly under the name of the Autumn Crocus, which name properly belongs to our blue Crocus nudiflorus.

A Gladiolus (G. illyricus) has recently been found in the New Forest, near Lyndhurst; it is worthy of culture, and indeed is, or was, a favourite plant in many gardens before it was discovered as a British plant, having come to our gardens from Southern Europe. The Spring Crocus (C. vernus) is abundant in the neighbourhood of Nottingham, and other parts of England and Ireland; and the less known but equally beautiful Autumn Crocus (C. nudiflorus) is also naturalized in Derbyshire, about Nottingham, and in a few other places. The Vernal Crocus is in nearly every garden, but the Autumnal Crocus is uncommon in gardens, and should be introduced to all, because it opens its handsome flowers when most others have perished. It is as easy of culture as the Spring Crocus, but, being so much scarcer, deserves good soil, and some watchfulness, to prevent its being dug up.

Those who have seen the Flowering Rush (Butomus umbellatus) in flower, are not likely to omit it from a collection of water-plants, as it is handsome and distinct. It is a native of the greater part of Europe and Asia, and the central and southern parts of England and Ireland. Plant it near the margin, it likes rich muddy soil. The common Sagittaria, frequent in England and Ireland, but not in Scotland, might be associated with this; and there is a very much finer double kind which is to be had here and there, and is probably a variety of the common kind.

Among picturesque plants for the water-side, nothing equals the great Water-dock (Rumex Hydrolapathum), which is rather generally dispersed over the British Isles, and has leaves quite sub-tropical in aspect and size, becoming of a lurid red in the autumn. It forms a fine mass of foliage on rich muddy banks. The Reed Maces (Typha) must not be forgotten, but they should not be allowed to run everywhere. The narrow-leaved one is more graceful than the common kind. Carex pendula is good for the margins of water, its drooping spikes being so distinct. It is rather common in

England, more so than Carex Pseudo-cyperus, which grows well in a foot or two of water, or on the margin of a muddy pond. Carex paniculata forms a strong and thick stem, sometimes 3 or 4 feet high, somewhat like a tree-fern, and with luxuriant masses of falling leaves, and on that account is transferred to moist places in gardens, though the larger specimens are difficult to remove and soon perish. Scirpus lacustris (the 'Bulrush') is too distinct a plant to be omitted, as its stems, sometimes attaining a height of more than 7 and even 8 feet, are very singular; Cyperus longus is also a handsome water-plant, reminding one of the aspect of the Papyrus when in flower. It is found in some of the southern counties of England. Cladium

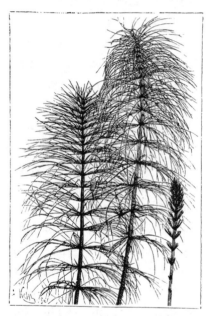

GIANT HORSE TAIL (Equisetum Telmateia).

Mariscus is also another distinct and rather scarce British aquatic which is worth a place.

The 'Great Horse-tail,' which grows pretty commonly in the greater part of England and Ireland, attains its greatest development in rich soil, reaching a height of four or five feet, and the numbers of slender branches depending from each whorl look most graceful. The wood Equisetum (E. sylvaticum), common all over Britain, is smaller, but even more graceful. The long simple-stemmed Equisetums, or Horse-tails, are also interesting to cultivate in marshy spots.

BRITISH WILLOWS.

Our Willows are as beautiful as Olives, perhaps much more beautiful, as after one has enjoyed their slender wands and silvery leaves against the summer sky they are the prettiest things in the winter landscape when they have lost all their leaves. Few even among the very men whose business it is to study trees, and plant them, i. e. landscape gardeners, have any idea of the noble effects that may be got by the artistic (i. e. natural) massing of our native willows, and their best varieties, in fitting situations. These occur often in this river-veined land, where there is so much marsh and estuary and shoreland, in which the hardy willows of our country and northern lands are at home. I say again, nothing in tropical or other lands is so effective in the landscape, so simple to secure, and so enduring as the pictures we may make from willows. Take the White Willow (Salix alba) alone— a stately and very large tree with its mass of silvery leaves so graceful in movement, and also a tree of much value for its timber. Around this tree, naturally grouped so to say, there are various forms of even greater value, of which the shoots assume yellow, red, and other hues—trees which are almost as large as the common White Willow in good soil by rivers, or in marsh land. But in effect and colour they are even more important, one of them, the scarlet form, glowing with splendid colour in the winter sun.

The better known yellow form (S. vitellina) is most delicate and charming in colour in the winter or in the sun after showers, and indeed in all lights. The colour in the summer is beautiful certainly, but it is the change from the silvery foliage of the summer to the bright decisive colour of winter that is so charming in this and its allies. Simply massed in groups, as things arrange themselves, these willows give us all we could desire in the way of pictures and beautiful effects in places where there is any breadth or expanse of marsh; but these great spaces are not necessary for single trees; Red and Yellow Willows may be grown in a small garden and be there beautiful. By putting in a few cuttings in the dykes of many farms these Willows will soon give a living picture.

Among British Willows there are some that claim our attention more than others. No doubt every one is interesting from the botanical point of view, but what we seek are effective and picturesque things that can take their place among the trees

WHITE WILLOW in Hampshire. (From drawing in possession of Lady Carnarvon.)

of the land, finer than any of which they are in colour.

The earliest flowering British Willow is what is called the Goat Willow, or 'pussies' by the children in spring. Next in importance is the Crack Willow or withy, which also becomes a very fine handsome tree nearly a hundred feet high, with a trunk sometimes twenty feet in girth, as in the specimen drawn by Alfred Parsons and engraved herein. There is a variety with the twigs orange or crimson in colour. The Bedford Willow also is a handsome tree and is supposed to be a hybrid between the White and the Crack Willow. The Goat Willow is not so handsome a tree as the others though precious for its beauty, but in almost every woodland district so common that there is no need to plant it. The Violet Willow is the next to claim our attention, being a graceful tree with violet shoots, very free and with a pretty grey bloom upon the leaves. Then we have the common Osier with its long wavy leaves silvery beneath—this willow is very common in wet places and in willow beds; it does not give us such beautiful trees as the White Willow in its various forms. Of the osier there are numerous varieties; and, lastly, we have the purple Osier, which is not quite a tree but a shrub attaining ten feet or so, with the advantage of being so bitter that rabbits will not eat it. Of this, as of all the others, there are various forms.

Although from a landscape point of view the best

are the tree willows, there is scarcely one which is not right by the water side; and for all who live in cool or mountain districts and have any kind of rock garden, the dwarf willows of our own mountains are charming, such as the Creeping Willow in its various forms, and the Woolly Willow, a dwarf silvery shrub of easy culture and a very pretty rock shrub: also the Netted Willow.

BRITISH ORCHIDS. Orchids everywhere beautiful and singular, whether showy, as in the hot or moist East, or tiny on the Kent and Surrey hills, where the Bee Orchis is often frequent,—it is most interesting to collect our native Orchids and to cultivate them. If we can succeed in growing the British Orchids, we are not likely to fail with any other hardy plants. They are the most difficult to cultivate, but amongst the most interesting things which can be grown. I have cultivated the Bee Orchis and the Fly Orchis and the Hand Orchis, and a number of other British Orchids, for several years, and flowered them annually. Devoting a small bed to their culture, in an open spot, digging some chalk into the bed, so as to give the plants the soil in which they are found most abundantly, I succeeded with all except those kinds that are parasitic on the roots of trees.

The difficulty was to imitate the state of the surface of the ground which exists where they live in a wild state. I knew that the surface-dressing of stunted, storm-beaten grass among which they nestle prevents

CRACK WILLOW in Kennet Valley.

the ground from cracking and drying, and also shelters the plants in winter—in short, keeps the surface open and healthy. To plant grass over a bed in a garden would not do, as the shelter and richness of the ground would induce it to grow so strong that unless we were to look after and shorten it very frequently there would be no chance of keeping it within bounds; and if we did not do that, it would soon smother all the Orchids. A good substitute is cocoa-fibre with a little sand to give it weight. An inch or two of this was spread over the bed, and it prevented cracking and evaporation, and kept the surface in a healthy state. The roots should be inserted firmly but without injuring their fibres—a great point. Few people know how to plant anything beyond a strong bedding plant.

If one of these Orchids which are accustomed to send their fleshy roots down into moist broken chalk in search of food were to be planted without care, it would soon perish.

Well, in this way I have grown and freely flowered the most curious and beautiful Bee Orchis, the Spider Orchis, the Fly Orchis, and a dozen others less difficult to cultivate. The marsh Epipactus palustris is one of the easiest native Orchids to cultivate, growing well in an artificial bog or moist border; whilst most of the Orchises will do well under the treatment above described. The Bee, Fly, and Spider Orchids belong to the genus Ophrys.

The common spotted Orchis (O. maculata), found

almost everywhere in the British Islands, is one of the freest to grow in a garden ; it makes large tufts of great beauty in stiff ground.   Lately nurserymen have been offering a plant described as a variety of this, under the name of O. maculata superba.   This is in reality the true British Orchis latifolia, a noble species, easy to grow in a moist spot, and having large spikes of bloom. O. militaris and O. fusca are among the handsomest of our Orchids ; but all are interesting, from the early spotted O. mascula to the Butterfly Orchis, both of which are of easy culture in a garden.   Perhaps the rarest and finest of all the British Orchids is the Lady's Slipper, nearly if not extinct.   Some of our nurserymen supply it, and they get their supplies from the Continent, where it is a widely distributed plant. It should be planted in broken limestone and fibrous loam, on the eastern side of a rockwork.   When well grown it is a beautiful plant, quite as much so as some of the Cypripediums grown in the Orchid house, but, being perfectly hardy, is far more interesting for the British garden.   The most important thing with regard to the Orchids is the procuring of them in a suitable state for planting.   When they are gathered in a wild state, the roots should be taken up as carefully as possible, and transferred to their garden home quickly and safely.   They are very often sold in markets, but the roots are mutilated, not only from careless taking up, but from being tightly bound with matting.

In the Grass family the common Ribbon Grass

(Phalaris arundinacea), Hierochloë borealis (a rare northern plant, sweet-scented when dried), Milium effusum (a handsome wood grass), the exquisitely graceful Apera Spica-venti of the eastern counties, the Hare's-tail Grass of the Channel Islands (Lagurus ovatus), the Quaking Grasses (Briza), the variegated Cock's-foot Grass, and Elymus arenarius, a stout grey grass, are interesting or beautiful.

OUR NATIVE POPLARS.

While there is little space to tell of all our native trees, many of which, in nature at least, are as well worthy our attention as any exotic ones, a few words on our native Poplars—among the hardiest of trees and the easiest to increase and grow—may not be amiss. When we think of the rapid growth and the good effect both of single trees and groups in the landscape, we find much to encourage us to plant Poplars—even our native kinds. They will grow in soils not so good for Oak or Ash or Pine, and this is important for a country like ours where there is so much swampy or low-lying land by rivers and estuaries, and also inland bog land, where the effect of Poplars will be beautiful and their growth profitable. The White Poplar or Abele, a native tree, is so fine in form and in all ways that it is not neglected, and about country houses we see noble trees of it nearly or quite one hundred feet high. It is excellent for planting by rivers and in spots likely to be under water betimes, and very handsome in the colour of the stems, especially where a number of old trees are seen picturesquely grouped. The Grey Poplar comes near this but is not so fine a tree I love our true native Aspen (P. tremula), best of all Poplars : though not uncommon in some underwoods, we rarely see it in England planted either as a garden or woodland tree— a great mistake, as in some countries of North Europe it is a large and useful tree, and always a beautiful one. There is a weeping form and one or two wild ones. The Black Poplar (P. nigra) is a tree of rapid growth and good effect in the landscape.

Our Native Evergreens.

When after a very hard winter we see the evergreen trees of the garden in mourning, and perhaps many of them dead, as happens to Laurels, Laurustinuses, and often even the Bay, it is a good time to consider the hardiness and other good qualities of our British ever-greens and the many forms raised from them. If we are fortunate enough to have old Yew trees near us, we do not find that a hard winter makes any difference to them, even winters that sear the evergreen Oak. We have collected within the past two hundred years evergreen trees from all parts of the northern world, but it is doubtful if any of them are better than the common Yew, which when old is often picturesque, and which lives green for a thousand years. Of this great tree we have many varieties, but none of them

THE BLACK POPLAR in the Kennet valley.

quite so good as the wild kind when old. In the garden little thought is given to the Yew, and it is crowded among shrubs; while in graveyards the roots are cut by digging, so that one seldom sees it in its fine character when old, which is very beautiful. The Golden Yew is a form of it, and there are other slight variegations which are interesting from a merely garden point of view. The Irish Yew is a well-known form; its prim shape is too often seen. Other seedling variations of the common Yew are better than the Irish variety.

After the ever-precious Yew, the best of our evergreen trees is the Holly, which in no country attains the beauty it does in our own; no evergreen brought over the sea is so valuable not only in its native form, often attaining forty feet even on the hills, but in the almost innumerable varieties raised from it, many of them being the best of all variegated shrubs in their silver and gold variegation; in fruit, too, it is the most beautiful of evergreens. Not merely as a garden tree is it precious, but as a most delightful shelter around fields for stock, in paddocks and places which we wish to shelter. A big wreath of unclipped Holly on the cold sides of fields is the best protection, and a grove of Holly north of any place we want to shelter is the best thing we can plant. As to the garden, we may make beautiful evergreen gardens of the forms of Holly alone; the only thing we have to fear are rabbits, which when numerous make Holly difficult to establish by

barking the little trees, and in hard winters even killing
many old trees.

Notwithstanding the many conifers brought from
other countries within the past few generations, it is
very doubtful if as regards beauty, more than one or
two equal our native Fir, which when old is so fine in
its stem and head. Few things in our country are more
picturesque than old groups and groves of the Scotch
Fir ; few indeed of the conifers we treasure from other
countries will ever give us anything so good as the
ruddy stems and frost-proof crests of this northern and
British tree.

Again, the best of evergreen climbers is our native
Ivy, and the many beautiful forms allied to it or that
have arisen from it. Ivy in our woods arranges
its own beautiful effects, but in gardens it might be
made more delightful use of. The form most commonly used in Britain—the Irish Ivy—is by no means
so graceful as some others, and there are a great
number of delightful kinds varying in form and even
in colour. These for edgings, banks, forming screens,
covering old trees, and forming summer-houses should
be made far larger use of. In many northern countries
our Ivy will not live in the open air, and it is so common
with us, that we rarely take advantage of our privileges
in such a possession in making bold shelters, wreaths,
and many beautiful things of it that would need little
care. It requires care in trimming when on our houses
and on cottage roofs ; but there are many pretty things

to make of it away from buildings, and among them Ivy-clad and Ivy-covered wigwams, summer-houses, and covered ways, the Ivy supported on a strong open frame-work, and trained over sticks and mats till it takes hold.

The Box tree, which is a true native on certain dry hills in the south of England, is so crowded in shrubberies, that one seldom sees its beauty as it is on the hills full in the sun, where the branches take a charming plumy toss. To wander among natural groves of Box is a great pleasure, and there is no reason why we should not plant it in groups or colonies by itself full in the sun, so that one might enjoy the same charm of form that it shows when wild. In some heavy soils it barely lives, but many soils suit it perfectly. A bower of one of the handsome-leaved Ivies in a grove of Box would be charming, and its charms would last long.

Also among our native evergreens is the common Juniper, a scrubby bush in some places, but on heaths in Surrey, and favoured heaths elsewhere, often growing over twenty feet high and very picturesque, especially where mingled with Holly. There is an upright form, called the Irish Juniper, in gardens.

The Arbutus, which borders nearly all the streams in Greece, ventures into Ireland, and is abundant there in certain parts in the south. This beautiful shrub, though tender in inland districts, is very precious for the seashore and mild districts, not only as an evergreen, but for the beauty of its flower and fruit. Still, it is the one British evergreen which has to be planted with discrimination in places where the winters are severe in inland districts.

We have thus glanced rapidly at the garden of British Wild Flowers and Trees, from showy Buttercups to modest Grasses; but it would require much greater space to do justice to the many delightful aspects of vegetation to which they give rise.

INDEX

————•————

Illustrations in Italics.

THE END

APPENDIX I
BOTANICAL REVISIONS
by Graham Stuart Thomas

38 Green Hellebore = *Helleborus foetidus*
41 Atragene alpina = *Clematis alpina*
44 Giant Scabious (Cephalaria procera) = *Cephalaria gigantea*
45 Giant Cow Parsnip = *Heracleum mantegazzianum*
47 Starwort = *Aster*
    Betonica = *Stachys*
    Funkia = *Hosta*
    Mulgedium = *Lactuca plumieri*
    Scolymus = *Cynara scolymus*
48 Teazle = *Dipsacus*
51 Hungarian Bindweed = *Calystegia pulchra*
52 Nootka Bramble = *Rubus nutkana*
    Aristolochia Sipho = *Aristolochia macrophylla*
53 Hardy Smilax = *Smilax aspera*
    Canadian Moonseed = *Menispermum canadense*
    Periwinkle = *Vinca*
    Speedwell = *Veronica*
    Globe Flower = *Trollius*
    Plume Fern (Struthiopteris) = *Matteuecia struthiopteris*
    Canadian Blood-root = *Sanguinaria canadensis*
    Winter Green (Pyrola) = *Gaultheria*
    May Apple = *Podophyllum peltatum*
    Common Myrrh = *Myrrhis odorata*
    Giant Fennel = *Ferula*
    May Flower = *Epigaea repens*
56 Quick = *Crataegus*
59 Cockspur Thorn = *Crataegus crus-galli*
    Cherry Plum = *Prunus cerasifera*
    Sloe = *Prunus spinosa*
64 Sweet Brier = *Rosa eglanteria*
    Dog Rose = *Rosa canina*
    Hazel = *Corylus avellana*

65 Crab = *Malus sylvestris*
   May Blossom (Quick) = *Crataegus oxyacantha*
   Clematis graveolens = *Clematis orientalis*
66 Moon Daisy = *Leucanthemum vulgare*
69 Virginian Creeper = *Parthenocissus quinquefolia*
72 Ampelopsis = *Parthenocissus*
77 Savin = *Juniperus sabina*
   Scotch Rose = *Rosa pimpinellifolia*
78 Compass Plant = *Silphium laciniatum*
   Evening Primrose = *Oenothera biennis*
   Globe Thistle = *Echinops*
   Golden Yarrow = *Achillea eupatorium*
82 Starwort = *Aster novi-belgii*, etc.
   French Willow = *Salix triandra*
   Blood-root = *Sanguinaria canadensis*
   Solomon's Seal = *Polygonatum* ✕*hybridum*
   Gold Thread = *Coptis trifoliata*
   Trailing Arbutus = *Arctostaphylos uva-ursi*, *A. nevadensis*
84 Skunk Cabbage = *Symplocarpus foetidus*
   Indian Poke = *Phytolacca*
   Marsh Marigold = *Caltha palustris*
88 Iris Kaempferi = *Iris ensata*
92 Woodruff = *Asperula odorata*
93 Poet's Narcissus = *Narcissus poeticus*
   Broad-leaved Saxifrage = *Bergenia*
95 Partridge Berry = *Gaultheria shallon*
   Indian Mountain Clematis = *Clematis orientalis*
98 Common Barberry = *Berberis vulgaris*
100 Herb Paris = *Paris quadrifolia*
101 Meadow-sweet = *Filipendula ulmaria*
102 Loosestrife = *Lythrum salicaria*
   Golden Rod = *Solidago*

102 Tritoma = *Kniphofia*
     Meadow-sweet, Red = *Filipendula purpurea*
103 Royal Fern = *Osmunda regalis*
107 Old White Double Rocket = *Hesperis matronalis* double form
111 Cardinal-flower = *Lobelia cardinalis*
112 Magnolia glauca = *Magnolia virginiana*
     Hibiscus, Herbaceous = *Hibiscus moscheutos*
114 Pyrenean Erinus = *Erinus alpinus*
115 Cheddar Pink = *Dianthus gratianopolitanus*
     Stonecrop = *Sedum*
     Houseleek = *Sempervivum*
     Rock Cress = *Aubrieta*
     Balearic Sandwort = *Arenaria balearica*
119 Sweet Brier = *Rosa eglanteria*
120 American Glossy Rose = *Rosa virginiana*
     Japan Rose = *Rosa rugosa*
     Carolina Rose = *Rosa caroliniana*
     Russian Wild Rose = *Rosa acicularis*
123 Wild Yellow Rose = *Rosa foetida*
130 Scilla campanulata = *Hyacinthoides hispanica*
131 Crane's Bill = *Geranium pratense*
     Honesty = *Lunaria annua*
132 Early Forget-me-not (Myosotis dissitiflora) = *Myosotis ramosissima*
134 Gout-weed = *Aegopodium podagraria* (ground elder)
135 Tiger Lily = *Lilium tigrinum*
138 Dielytra spectabilis = *Dicentra spectabilis*
     Tree Paeony = *Paeonia suffruticosa*
     Spiraea Aruncus = *Aruncus dioicus*
139 Welsh Poppy = *Meconopsis cambrica*
     Sun Rose = *Helianthemum*
     Rock Rose = *Cistus*

Spanish Broom = *Spartium junceum*

Balm = *Melissa officinalis*

158 Arundinaria falcata = *Chimonobambusa falcata*

Bambusa viridis-glaucescens = *Phyllostachys viridiglaucescens*

Bambusa Metake = *Pseudosasa japonica*

165 Dielytra = *Dicentra*

166 Dianthus caesius = *Dianthus gratianopolitanus*

168 Menziesia polifolia = *Daboecia cantabrica*

170 Funkia coerulea = *Hosta ventricosa*

Siebold's Plantain Lily = *Hosta sieboldiana*

171 Oak Fern = *Gymnocarpium dryopteris*

Beech Fern = *Gymnocarpium phegopteris*

172 Geranium Armenum = *Geranium psilostemon*

174 Hemerocallis flava = *Hemerocallis lilio-asphodelus*

178 Lathyrus pyrenaicus = *Lathyrus sylvestris*

180 Molopospermum cicutarium = *Molopospermum peloponnesiacum*

182 Bitter Vetch = *Vicia ervilea*

183 Star of Bethlehem = *Ornithogalum umbellatum*

184 Polygonum cuspidatum, P. Sachalinense = *Fallopia japonica, F. sachalinensis*

186 Phytolacca decandra = *Phytolacca americana*

Pyrethrum serotinum = *Leucanthemella serotina*

Rosa berberifolia = *Rosa persica*

188 Rosa microphylla rubra plena = *Rosa roxburghii* 'Roxburghii'

Spiraea venusta = *Filipendula rubra* 'Venusta'

Spiraea palmata = *Filipendula purpurea*

Spiraea aruncus = *Aruncus dioicus*

190 Hyacinthus amethystinus = *Brimeura amethystina*

191 Megasea = *Bergenia*

193 Telekia cordifolia = *Buphthalmum speciosum*

Tritoma = *Kniphofia*

198 Dielytra = *Dicentra*
   Tunica Saxifraga = *Petrorhagia saxifraga*
   Waldsteinia trifolia = *Waldsteinia ternata*
   Saxifraga crassifolia = *Bergenia crassifolia*
   Athamanta Matthioli = *Athamanta turbith*
   Veronica Candida = *Veronica spicata* subsp. *incana*
   Zietenia lavandulaefolia = *Stachys lavandulifolia*
   Polygonum Brunonis, P. vaccinifolium = *Persicaria affinis,*
   P. vacciniifolium

199 Spiraea Aruncus = *Aruncus dioicus*
   Alfredia cernua = *Carduus*
   Helianthus orgyalis = *Helianthus salicifolius*
   Harpalium rigidum = *Helianthus rigidus*
   Althaea taurinensis = *Althaea officinalis*
   Aralia japonica = *Fatsia japonica*
   Aralia edulis = *Aralia cordata*
   Anemone japonica = *Anemone* ×*hybrida*

203 Ficaria grandiflora = *Ranunculus ficaria*
   Scilla campanulata = *Hyacinthoides hispanica*
   Cypripedium spectabile = *Cypripedium reginae*
   Funkia grandiflora = *Hosta plantaginea* 'Grandiflora'

204 Othonna = *Othonnopsis*
   Vittadenia triloba = *Erigeron mucronatus*
   Dorycnium sericeum = *Dorycnium hirsutum*
   Nepeta Mussinii = *Nepeta* ×*faassenii*
   Plumbago Larpentae = *Ceratostigma plumbaginoides*
   Stachys lanata = *Stachys byzantina*

205 Campanula pumila = *Campanula cochleariifolia*
   Koniga maritima = *Lobularia maritima*
   Trichomanes = *Asplenium trichomanes*
   Alyssum maritimum = *Lobularia maritima*
   Amberboa moschata = *Centaurea moschata*

206 Merendera Bulbocodium = *Merendera montana*
Trichonema = *Romulea*

209 Androsaemum officinale = *Hypericum androsaemum*

210 Large-leaved Rockfoil = *Bergenia*

214 Water Crowfoots = *Ranunculus hederaceus, R. tripartitus*

216 Robinson Blue Windflower = *Anemone nemorosa*
'Robinsoniana'

217 Pasque Anemone = *Pulsatilla vulgaris*

220 White Water Lily = *Nymphaea alba*

221 Horned Poppy = *Glaucium*

222 Seakale = *Crambe maritima*

222 Milkwort = *Polygala*

225 Restharrow = *Ononis repens*
Bird's-foot Trefoil = *Lotus corniculatus*

226 Spiraea filipendula = *Filipendula ulmaria*

228 Rosa spinosissima = *Rosa pimpinellifolia*

231 Rosa rubiginosa = *Rosa eglanteria*
Crataegus oxyacantha = *Crataegus laevigatus*

233 Pyrus torminalis = *Sorbus torminalis*
Pyrus Aria = *Sorbus aria*
Pyrus latifolia = *Sorbus latifolia*

234 Pyrus scandica = *Sorbus intermedia*
Pyrus hybrida = *Sorbus hybrida*
Pyrus Aucuparia = *Sorbus aucuparia*
Pyrus Malus = *Malus*
Germanica = *Mespilus germanica*

246 Villarsia nymphaeoides = *Nymphoides peltata*

249 Mountain Everlasting (Gnaphalium dioicum) = *Antennaria dioica*
Ivy Campanula (C. hederacea) = *Wahlenbergia hederacea*

251 Armeria vulgaris = *Armeria maritima*

253 Convallaria bifolia = *Maianthemum bifolium*

261 Goat Willow = *Salix caprea*
     Crack Willow = *Salix fragilis*
     Violet Willow = *Salix daphnoides*
     Osier = *Salix viminalis*
     Purple Osier = *Salix purpurea*
262 Creeping Willow = *Salix repens*
     Woolly Willow = *Salix lanata*
267 White Poplar = *Populus alba*
     Grey Poplar = *Populus canescens*
268 Yew = *Taxus*
271 Holly = *Ilex*
272 Ivy = *Hedera*
273 Box = *Buxus*

APPENDIX II

Material Supplied by William Robinson for the Proposed
Eighth Edition of 1932

ORIGIN OF THE WILD GARDEN

As to the origin of my ideas of the Wild Garden, I think they first occurred to me along the banks of the Southern Railway between East Grinstead and West Hoathly. Sometimes when I went through the station I had a pocketful of seeds of some bush or plant which I used to scatter about, usually forgetting all about them afterwards, but most certainly they all came up again. These adorned the banks for some time, but the powers in the office decreed that all bushes and plants along the banks were to be destroyed, and so mine perished, but I think the roots are there yet.

The late Mr. Joseph Turner, a much trusted wood-surveyor of the region, told me that the best soil in England for growing oaks—I mean as regards quality, not as regards size—was to be found on those hills of ours between Tunbridge Wells and Horsham. Some twenty years ago I got seeds of large oaks and scattered them about without cover, not in the Forest but almost on the edge of it, and this led me to think that the same thing might be carried out in the Forest itself. To see our native trees in their full majesty of growth, a thing to be much desired, the crowded wood or copse does not always meet our wants. The essential thing for young and old is to see our native trees in their full stature and developed beauty.

In any case I had this in my mind for some years after coming here, but I had so much to do with making roads and planting my own things I could not attend to it. But since then I have been carefully over the whole area and found out what native plants are absent, or planted so sparsely as to be almost absent. In all I found sixteen kinds of native plants, shrubs and trees were missing.

IN ASHDOWN FOREST

It is my happy fate to find myself on land not on Ashdown Forest, but near. The Forest is a noble remnant of old days: the shooting place of the Normans who were not gentle in their ways; and now it is a very precious piece for the South of England and particularly Sussex. Miles along and across, an airy stretch of land with fine roads, but hardly any trees although it is called a Forest. Even the Scotch fir which should be in it in groups and shelters is in starved dots, miles apart.

As to the vegetation, the commonest is our native furze which is everywhere and burns itself and everything near. There is no control of any kind, and the sheep and lambs get all black rubbing against its burnt stems. Not the slightest care is taken to lessen its ravages. I wrote and told the Commissioners of the Forest to restrict its area to, say, one hundred acres or more, root up the rest and lay the turf down in grass.

There are few deer to be seen, but it might easily nourish a herd or two of these creatures with enough food to keep them at home. As it is, the furze has it all to itself; you see nothing else for acres at a time but blackened furze all year round.

After many years on the Forest I find that the following

trees are often missing, or, if not missing, used in too slight a way:

White Willow, *Salix alba.* —I doubt if any native tree has given me more pleasure in storm and rain than the White Willow. It is hardy with us and throughout much of Europe. A man I trusted much advised me to plant a large group of it near my old Hammer Pond, and I think it is always better grouped than dotted about. In our Isles generally there is much marshy ground in which it might well be planted, not forgetting its use for the cricket field. The main variety is said to be the one best liked for this purpose, but I found out from my own buyers in the woods that they never refused the common white willow.

Red Dogwood, *Cornus alba.* —This is a brilliant shrub, and though a native of Siberia it takes to our land very readily and is of easy culture and propagation. We have had it a long time in our country and thoroughly tested it. For hollow and marshy places it cannot be surpassed for effect. I am rather fond of it, and have planted a good deal; a curious little trait about it is that when planted in very weedy ground with strong docks and thistles, after some years it makes such a close canopy over the ground that the weeds give up the fight and totally disappear. You may call it a weed-killer!

Ash, *Fraxinus excelsior.* —In beauty and stately form no British tree strikes me so much as this, at least in our Sussex ground. It is a splendid tree with many uses, but a curious thing about it is that it is not always best as wood where it grows best. Rabbits are very apt to injure it if [it is] not protected.

May or **Whitethorn,** *Crataegus oxyacantha.* —This lovely tree is finest to some extent massed in good numbers, as in the Phoenix Park, Dublin. There are single and double forms, but these hardly come into the rough and ready way of Forest planting, [though] I think the single form deserves to be planted a good deal. The birds come in swarms from the icy North and like the fruit very well.

Apple, *Malus communis.* —This is the common wild stock from which our apples have come down to us for generations form every country in Europe, but now we are dealing with the Forest and therefore only the wild tree should be thought of. It is very beautiful.

Pear, *Pyrus communis.* —The pear is a very beautiful tree but rather neglected by gardeners. It is really a forest tree, very tall and stately in its wild form, and so doesn't come into our prime stock in the garden, but in a Forest like this, it should have a good place. In bloom it is earlier than the apple, and quite as beautiful. The fruit of the wild pear is never, like that of the wild apple, eatable, but it is worth growing for its beauty.

Sycamore, *Acer pseudo-platanus.* —Treated almost as a weed in some countries where it sheds its seed so freely, it is really a very noble tree. It is to be seen in a fine state at Knowle and other places in Sussex. The timber is also very valuable so I have often sown it, with many other things, in the Forest.

Lime, *Tilia platyphyllos.* —We are lucky in having one lime hardy on our land and that is Tilia platyphyllos, of which there certainly should be a group in the Forest.

Maple, *Acer campestre.* —This is the field maple, common in the hedge rows in England and occasionally a fine tree. It should be encouraged in the Forest.

Broom, *Spartium junceum.* —Perhaps the handsomest of our native bushes. It is most striking seen singly or in small groups. For effect and beauty it cannot be surpassed as a forest plant.

Whitebeam, *Pyrus aria.* —This is a medium-sized tree which gives good effect in the Spring in the woods. It is characteristic of our chalky soil in Spring.

Mountain Ash, Rowan, *Pyrus aucuparia.* —A handsome wild thing in many parts of our Island and Europe. It is common everywhere and I have planted much of it about here.

Spindle-tree, *Euonymus europaeus.* —This native shrub is a very beautiful thing to have in Autumn days. I think the wood, in our days, is much used in the kitchen, and from this use it gets its name.

Common Barberry, *Berberis vulgaris.* —In recent days we have witnessed very many Barberries coming from very many parts of the cold, north earth, but after growing them all I had to confess that this was as pretty as any of them. I did not know it myself until one day, near an old house in Warwickshire, I saw a whole mass of it in fruit, and it struck me very much. Its purple form differs only in the colour of the leaf, and is also a beautiful plant.

The Royal Fern, *Osmunda regalis.* —This most famous of native plants is not usually made the most of in the Forest. The dealers of London, in fact, take it and sell it to people and it dies in their back-yards! A common plant in Southern England and Ireland, it is rarely made effective use of as regards its beauty. The late Doctor Evershed Wallis told me that when he came first to the Forest the cattle used to go for shade amongst this plant, but the London hawkers settled all that by digging it up. In my own place here there must have been a number of these plants grown, as we found some tiny seedlings in a shaw in one of the fields. In the Forest at present there is no sign of it, and of course one of the duties of the coming men is to see that it is not only to be found frequently, but in the best conditions. One day, returning from my first sight of the Cedars of Lebanon in a wild state, I passed through some great oak woods with many of the Royal Fern in them, in, or near, springs, and superb in their effect in the silent woods. Much of North Africa is wooded country, and as the climate is fairly similar to ours, the Royal Fern is quite happy there and grows several feet high. It should be an easy task to scatter its seeds round about watery places in the Forest, and I feel it becomes part of my duty to sow these seeds in all likely places, and the rest, as the Arabs say, 'is in the hands of God'.

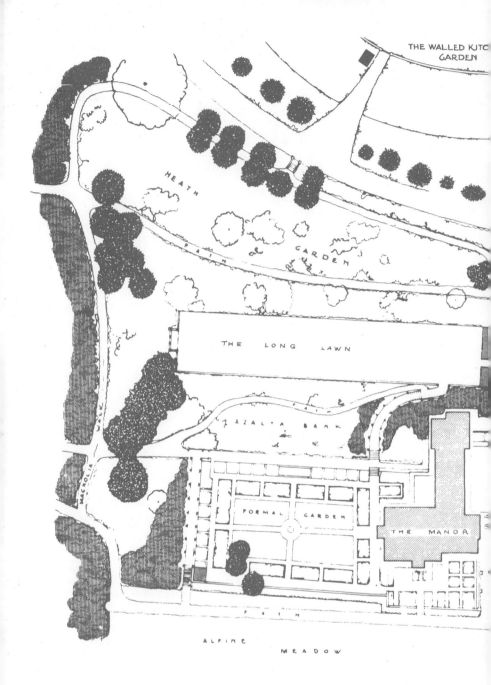

THE WALLED KITCHEN
GARDEN

HEATH

GARDEN

PATH

THE LONG LAWN

PATH

AZALEA BANK

MAGNOLIA WALK

FORMAL GARDEN

THE MANOR

PATH

ALPINE MEADOW